Amir Arooni (CIO, NN): 'Learn dilemmas, and also being criti critical themes in this book. I makers, and to those who wan rapidly changing world!'

Svenja de Vos (Director of Transformation, Tele2 AB): 'An easy to read book that induces self-reflection and the energy to change!'

Teun van der Vorm (CIO, ANWB): 'An inspiring book in which the methods and practical lessons gained from Mark's grandfather taught me to grasp how to successfully work with self-managing teams. Directly applicable!'

Johan van Hall (Vice President, Board of Directors and COO, ABNAMRO Group): 'Thanks to this book, I've learned a lot in a short amount of time with regard to shepherds and beekeepers, and thereby got the insight that the biggest challenge is to change yourself, first.'

Lisette Oosterbroek (Vice President Innovation Excellence KPN): 'The Bee Shepherd describes a journey. Not only a journey for the main character, but also for you as the reader. Inspiring, fascinating, and liberating!'

Nico Orie (Global Director, HR Operations, AkzoNobel): 'A management book, but with a twist. The Bee Shepherd gives original insights into leadership of self-managing teams.'

John Heideman (Head Support & Process Management, ING): 'This book helps you to understand how you can execute Agile self-organization more successfully by changing your old style of management and learning from the bee shepherd.'

Alfred de Vries (Executive Director, Operations and Development, CRV): 'Recognizable lessons for directing professionals brought to light in an original way.'

Frans van der Horst (CIO, ABNAMRO Group): 'Managers with shut-up-get-out-I-have-always-done-it-this-way syndrome are the greatest obstacle to attaining self-managing teams and better outcomes for customers. This is laid out very sharply in this book!'

Peter Groen (Head of IT Strategy, Security, and Control, NIBC Bank): 'From the rush of ad hoc troubleshooting to the enjoyment of true collaboration and the results it produces. This book provides valuable insights for anyone who wants to sustainably improve by laying the foundation for Agile.'

Ronald Dähne (Technology Director of Cloud Solutions, Exact): 'This parable of bees and the shepherd helps you to simply and clearly make the right choices when working with self-managing teams.'

Tino Scholman (Vice President of Cloud, Oracle EMEA): 'This is a wonderful book. It explains aptly that 'Lean' is easily within reach. The job of a beekeeper is not to interfere with the work of the bees, but to ensure that they can execute their work.'

Rini van Solingen

How to lead self-managing teams?

Changing leadership from sheepherding to beekeeping

– A Business Novel –

Published by Rini van Solingen, printed by CreateSpace

© 2016 – All Rights Reserved – by Rini van Solingen

Publisher: Rini van Solingen
Printed by CreateSpace, an Amazon.com company

ISBN 978 15 376 3903 1

Content

Foreword 7

1. To the Island 13
2. Grandpa Marcus 23
3. Shearing Bees 37
4. Lex 49
5. Cabinets and Frameworks 63
6. Order, Structure, and Chaos 79
7. More by Doing Less 87
8. Getting Stung 101
9. Back to the Island 117

The Bee-Shepherd Model 123

Epilogue 135
Acknowledgements 139
About The Author 143

Foreword

When Rini asked me to write this foreword, I briefly had my doubts. This book is namely mostly about self-management, which to me is just a means to an end. Self-management must always serve a higher purpose: communally solving an existing problem as well as possible; and the realization of an extraordinary connection with your surroundings. In many cases, self-management leads to good solutions that have been reached quickly and locally. But it remains a tool. Self-management is not a goal in and of itself.

Self-management is also not exactly new; it existed in the 1980's. During that time, I was a nurse. The work was varied in nature and there were constant appeals to utilize one's creativity in the workplace. So many different problems and so many different solutions. Every day was an adventure with children, young mothers, and the elderly. The work was embedded in daily life; you were a part of the community, which motivated you to work quite effectively.

All that changed in the 1990's. Politicians thought that economies of scale would lead to more efficient healthcare for patients. Residential care organizations merged and evolved into massive organization that had ambitions of 'succeeding.' I could not tolerate this management style of thinking in health care; the notion that there are people who think, the managers, and that there are other people to execute, the employees. That thought process of thinking from top to bottom; I find it dramatic. At that point, the perspective has changed from thinking about the client to the needs of the organization. That's why I quit in 1993.

But it the end, it remained on my mind. Therefore, ten years ago my wife and I started Buurtzorg Foundation. Our organization provides personal care and nursing care to the homes of clients who are seriously ill, returning home from a hospital stay, or who want to continue living independently. Buurtzorg is customized based upon each client's possibilities and circumstances. Every client receives a personal counselor who helps to examine the client's anticipated care needs now and in the future. We solve problems locally. We do this in a way that works best for everyone and which also does justice to all parties involved: the local policeman, doctor or neighbor, and the sister that lives around the corner.

Buurtzorg works with small teams of district nurses and caretakers. These are self-managing teams that cater to the specific wishes and needs of each individual client. In this way, our employees own the solution. These are their clients, their neighborhood, their office, and their team. Therefore we have no managers or public relations department at Buurtzorg. The employees' skills and expertise and the personal relationship with the client are at the center. Clients are satisfied and require a lower duration of care on average.

We started Buurtzorg at that time with a small team of four employees. We now count more than 880 teams, more than 9,700 employees, and have reached an annual revenue of $357 Million Dollars.

The lessons in this book work. I have been able to experience this myself. And these strategies work not only in healthcare, but also in many other industries. Allowing the people who do the work to organize it themselves is possible anywhere. Moreover, it renders various types of management roles and coordinator roles unnecessary. You can use it anywhere: in education, in police work, in the banking world. Let the people who execute the work self-organize. They can do it better than you would think. Rely on their knowledge, insight, and skill. Only in this way can you let people perform at their best and develop their skills.

'The less you organize, the better it is!' is then my main message. Trust and responsibility instead of control and suspicion. This book provides an accessible and clear understanding of the reasons why self-managing teams are the basis for work in the 21st century. It is ideal for folks who want to learn more about self-organization and harness it to help them reach their goals. In short: a must read!

Jos de Blok
Director, Buurtzorg Foundation[*]

---

[*]Buurtzorg Foundation is a prominent case in the Frederic Laloux book: Reinventing Organizations (Nelson Parker, 2014).

How to lead self-managing teams?

– A Business Novel –

1. To the Island

It is half past seven at night when Mark Vandenburg walks through the sliding doors of his office building, on the way to his car. It's still a one-and-a-half hour drive to the port, and the last boat leaves promptly at ten past nine; he only has ten minutes of leeway. A short vacation to his grandfather's island lies in the distance.

It's been a few years since he's been there last, and given that his grandfather never leaves the island anymore, they haven't seen each other in a while. Every now and then they do check in on the phone. They talk about the weather, the dike, and the water. And of course how busy it always is on the island, since it seems like more and more tourists are coming each year.

This week, Mark is going alone. Originally his girlfriend Susan had planned to come with, but had to cancel at the last minute. She's an integration coach and works in a tight-knit team. One of her direct colleagues had to leave the country for a week quite suddenly – something to do with her family. Because of this, the rest of her colleagues couldn't pick up the slack alone and Susan had to jump in to help.

Mark and she had had a heated conversation about it. Susan had proposed to leave one week later, but that wasn't an option for Mark. An arrangement is an arrangement, he thought; so he decided to go alone after all.

***

It ended up still being a rather hectic day at the office. At the large supermarket chain where he works, he's responsible for maintaining the company's IT systems and ensuring that they are fully functional. Mark has the feeling that his job has become increasingly crucial the last few years. It seems as if nothing can happen in the company without help from his department. They're involved in everything, whether it's the stocking of store locations, order processing, the check-out process, or helping with staffing; it doesn't matter. There's always an underlying system that supports the process. More and more things seem to revolve around Mark's division when it comes to new developments. Meanwhile, he also has to make sure that the existing systems stay up and running. It all keeps him quite busy.

Today was another one of those days. Halfway through the morning, he received a panicked phone call from the distribution center. The program that prepares orders for the stores kept getting stuck. This caused a huge delay in collecting the orders, and by the end of the day there was a long line of trucks idling and waiting, because things were moving far too slowly in the distribution center.

On the one hand, it is his great frustration that he dared to take on days like this one, which emphasized how scarce deep knowledge of the company is, and how little his own people dare to take action. At the same time, it is also very satisfying to him. The thrill when everything is working again, when the systems are back online and the danger has subsided. That adrenaline rush is almost addictive, in a sense. Every time when the problems are sky high and nobody really knows where to start or where the dysfunction resides; that's when Mark is at his best. These qualities must have earned him a fortune. Year after year he receives laudatory performance reviews, with the corresponding salary increases and title changes reflecting his high value. His own office complete with a personal secretary, Joyce, and his own parking spot; it's all a part of the deal.

He doesn't have to walk far to get to his car, an Aston Martin convertible that he bought recently with some trepidation. Although it's not brand new, he still hesitated. Is that okay to do at a supermarket? What will the truck drivers have to say about it? Eventually he decided to do it; he indeed works hard enough for it, he thought. And when he tours across the island with the top down, it gives him an incalculable feeling of freedom.

He smoothly steers his car through the gates of the office lot exit. As he passes by, he gives a quick greeting to the guard and consequently zooms toward the highway. Luckily there's not really any traffic around this time, and by cruising at 85 miles per hour he makes it on the last ferry with time to spare.

***

At half past eight, Mark is standing on the deck of the ferry. He bought a large cup of coffee and goes to sit on one of the benches. It's a fantastic evening. The sun hangs low above the ocean, emitting a beautiful deep orange color as it sinks past the horizon. He feels his body relax. The stress of the day melts away like snow in front of the sun.

And there's plenty of stress at the office. Just to have some vestige of control, he's at the office every day around seven o'clock. And the days that he's on time for dinner are few and far between. It's slowly starting to break him down. Every year he resolves to do things differently: to delegate more, to spread more responsibility to his team, so that he can take a step back from the daily routine and focus himself more on the big picture and the future. To serve as a better leader. But somehow, it never really pans out.

At the moment, there's a plan of change in his company centered around self-managing teams. The company must become agile. The CEO has made himself responsible for implementing this change. Agility, responsiveness, and speed are the new paradigm. Achieving this combination is really what everything is about in some way or another. Everyone is placed in fixed teams with each other and the new teams are instructed to function by organizing themselves, making decisions autonomously, and acting quickly and decisively. That would provide the desired speed and agility.

As an idea, it makes sense to Mark. In principle, he's a huge proponent of delegating more, especially since having to be personally involved in solving operational problems is not a sustainable solution. But unfortunately, he doesn't observe these self-managing teams functioning well in practice. On paper it all seems quite reorganized and lean, but in practice things are still moving slowly. And that's logical; it's new. Often, there are still many situations where it's unclear to everyone what exactly is expected of them. There's not a weekend that goes by without him being called several times. They still always ask Mark for permission and have difficulty making their own decisions and acting decisively.

He often wonders about it and has myriad questions. How does that work, leading self-managing teams? When am I doing it the right way? How do I stay in control? What should I and should I not be involved with? Do I have other tasks? And if so, which ones? Where do I lay the balance between granting autonomy and monitoring things? Why should I not intervene if something is likely to go wrong, and why should I let my teams make what I know to be mistakes? It's not efficient, and a waste of money. How can you expect the team to feel the same degree of responsibility as me? These are questions to which Mark has yet to find an answer.

***

That morning, Mark's departure from his house felt rather stiff. Susan was not happy that Mark is going alone, and she made sure he noticed as much. Mark tried to ignore her aloof attitude and body language. After a while, he broke the silence: "how about that, this time you're the one choosing to go to work; not me." Mark held back from commenting on her excuse, namely that she had no choice. He shook his head and as he caught a glance at Susan's reddening face, he figured he should probably leave it at that. With one swift motion, she slammed the door behind her as she darted towards her office.

Deep in his heart, Mark wishes that Susan would stay home. He feels that their fifteen year old daughter Mandy is actually a bit too young to stay home alone. Unsurprisingly, Mandy isn't too enthusiastic about the idea. So in a way, it calms him to know that Susan isn't joining him. She always thinks Mark doesn't let her go out much, that he's coddling her and gives her far too few responsibilities. After all, she is "already" fifteen, according to Susan. It is a recurring topic prompting conflict between them.

Consequently, Mark goes alone. On his own, he can enjoy himself plenty. He likes hiking alone since he has all the time to let his mind run free. And mountain biking isn't exactly Susan's cup of tea. She would much rather read two novels a day, a not uncommon occurrence.

***

Mark quietly takes a big gulp of coffee while he enjoys the beautiful sunset. As the ferry lurches along, he feels his problems disappearing with the sun behind the horizon. It's as if he starts feeling the tranquility of the island as soon as the ferry sets off, he ponders. It's amazing how the pace of life on an island seems to be twice as slow compared to the shore.

Mark had missed that feeling, and he had only just realized it moments ago. Ever since his parents came back to the shore, he seldom finds himself on the island anymore. It's also been about fifteen years since they moved. Right before Mandy's birth, they had moved to come live in the neighborhood. Nevertheless, Mark has a more special relationship with his grandfather Marcus. He's named after him, actually: Marcus Emanuel Vandenburg, that's his official name. His parents always called him 'Marcus Jr.' but when he started High School, he had changed it to Mark, with a 'k.' His parents and grandfather tacitly went along with it.

Mark was born on the island and lived there his entire youth. He went to the shore to go to college. During the first year, he came back every week, with a bag full of dirty laundry. And of course, he was on the island all summer. But after his second year of study, he began returning less frequently, so much so that he didn't even go back for vacations during the last two years. He landed a solid job, and then bought a house. In this way, he left the island step by step. A quite typical story, allegedly.

Ultimately, it's now been three years since he's been back on the island. He doesn't come there enough. But it really is his island; it's in his blood, or so he strongly feels. Even when he's taking the ferry out there for the first time in years. Why does he go so little? How could he have forgotten this feeling?

***

From the dock, it's a fifteen minute drive to his Aunt Ronda's house. She lives right next to grandpa and insisted that he stay with her. Aunt Ronda had previously taken over his parents' house when they eventually left the island. She doesn't have any kids, and she's been a widow for more than ten years. She takes very good care of grandpa. Sometimes a little too well, according to grandpa. Every time he calls Mark, he complains about her meddling. Mark always laughs about it. Grandpa couldn't take care of himself without Aunt Ronda, and he knows that. And Aunt Ronda knows it too.

Mark entertained the idea of still grabbing a hotel instead. He knows how fond Aunt Ronda is of visitors and he really doesn't want to be patronized all day and forced to fill her need for companionship. At the same time, that didn't feel right either. After all, it is also his own family's home.

Aunt Ronda is waiting for him already. Mark sees her thin face and beady eyes piercing through the curtains as he parks his car. After a friendly greeting with a slightly excessively wet kiss, they drink a cup of tea together. She questions him constantly about Susan and Mandy. Mark is surprised at all of the things his Aunt knows to ask about. She really wants to know everything about his daughter, but even Mark doesn't know the answers to most of her questions. And he doesn't want to tell her about Mandy's problems at school. Then she wouldn't talk about anything else. Mark quickly drinks his tea and politely turns down a second cup; he's had a long day behind him and he wants to go to bed.

By eleven o'clock he walks into his former bedroom. With his smartphone, he shoots a quick text message to the home front: *"Hey honey. Still angry? Mandy OK? Was able to get the last boat. Aunt Ronda is still Aunt Ronda, hahaha. I'll call you tomorrow, if that's alright ;-) xxx."*

Mark then turns off the light. Although he would have preferred to lie next to Susan, he can now sleep with the window wide open. One of the delights of being away from home. Susan always gets cold, so the windows always have to stay shut.

A cool breeze circulates through his bedroom. He smells the island. That unique combination of grass and ocean mist that you only find in one place: home! For a moment, he realizes how quiet it is outside. Even with the window open. However, he fails to listen much longer as he sinks into a deep slumber after a few minutes.

2. Grandpa Marcus

The next morning, Mark is up rather early; the power of habit. At quarter past five, he's already standing next to his bed. He quickly puts on his clothes and hiking boots. There's nothing more beautiful than a sunrise on the southeast side of the island. From Aunt Ronda's house it's just a ten minute walk to the dike. Mark starts the day with a substantial walk. He breathes in the fresh air, listens to the seagulls, and looks at the waves.

On the dike, he looks first at the sunrise. The sky is beautiful, containing clouds of all sorts of colors. Purple, orange, dark blue. Stunning. He keeps taking photos of it all. Eventually, he forces himself to put his phone away so that he can be fully focused on enjoying the sunrise. On the way back, he takes a detour to the ferry. They rent bikes there, and thankfully he had instructed Joyce, his secretary, to reserve a beautiful mountain bike.

When he rides through the village moments later, he watches as the owner of the village's town hall places a billboard outlining today's specials on the sidewalk—she's about to open. Nowadays the town hall has a tea room inside it. Mark decides to have breakfast there; a croissant, fresh orange juice, and a double espresso. He reads the newspaper leisurely, and orders a second coffee.

It's already half past ten when he parks his bike on the side of Aunt Ronda's house. She doesn't look too happy. With her grey hair in a bun like always and her accusatory gaze, she reminds Mark of a strict schoolteacher. "I've been waiting on you for breakfast since seven thirty!" she says somewhat curtly. "At first I thought you were still asleep, but when you still weren't down by eight thirty I decided to go take a look. But you were already gone!"

Mark replies: "Sorry Aunt Ronda, I'm an early bird! I've already been for a walk, watched the sunrise from the dike, and picked up my mountain bike. And then I had breakfast in the town hall. So nice to have breakfast while reading the newspaper. I didn't expect that. But I think it would be best if you take into account that I won't be eating breakfast here. I want to do a lot of biking and walking, both of which I usually do early!"

"Oh," she says, clearly crestfallen. "Really? I had already boiled eggs and baked fresh bread for you. Do you really not want to have breakfast? I have no problems with waking up early, by the way! Then it will be ready for you at five thirty. That's no problem whatsoever! Are you really sure?"

Mark puts his arm around her and gives her a kiss on her forehead. She means it all so well. "No, Aunt Ronda, that's really sweet of you, but I'm never hungry around that time. Normally I only eat when I get to the office. Just don't worry about it. I really like that I can stay here, but one thing I really love about being on vacation means that I can do my own thing. I had considered getting a room in the hotel in the village down the way. So that you won't be sitting around, waiting for a guest who usually isn't home, I fully understand. In that case I would just move to the hotel."

"Are you crazy?" She responds decisively. "You are not going in that hotel. This is your home, and you will sleep here. That's that. Grandpa is always complaining that I'm such a dominating mother hen. But it's definitely not helping to be doing everything alone, either. I'm really glad that you're here and that it's not so quiet in the house. So I will restrain myself and not make you breakfast. But then I do expect you to dine with Grandpa and me in the evenings!"

"Sounds good," Mark answers. "I'm going to take a quick shower and then head over to see Grandpa."

Aunt Ronda calls after him: "Make sure you ask whether he's taken his red pills!"

***

At ten o'clock, Grandpa is sitting is his usual spot at the table. With a fresh pot of coffee, he would always peruse the local newspaper. He reads the newspaper from front to back, and then from back to front for good measure. His long, gray hair is tied behind his head in a ponytail, so that it doesn't get in the way while he's reading. Grandpa has always had long hair. Even at his age, it gives him a lively appearance.

"So, Marcus Junior," he grumbles as Mark walks into the room. "Could you still find it? It's been too long since you've been on the island, and I was expecting you for coffee much earlier!"

"Well, Grandpa, what a hearty welcome," Mark replied cynically. "Don't grumble like that. Should I go away, otherwise? But there is some truth to what you're saying. It has been too long, and I also realize that I've missed the island." He walks to his Grandpa, who reluctantly gets up, to embrace him. He gives Mark a kiss on the cheek and sits down again.

"Don't forget: once an islander, always an islander. You can't escape that. You can try to hide it and forget about it, but you'll never forget what you know. As the saying goes, 'East, West, home is best!'"

"You're right," Mark replied. "I had forgotten how peaceful the island is. This is going to be a week of old-fashioned relaxation; of that much I'm sure!"

"Well then, go ahead and have a seat," Grandpa says. "And drink your coffee!", as he folds his cold, wrinkled hands around his coffee mug to warm them.

Grandpa asks first about the situation at home. About Susan and of course his granddaughter Mandy. After that, they talk about the news.

Grandpa always looks at the obituaries first; that's a given. "Let's check out the losers," he says jokingly. "The older you get, the more acquaintances of yours are in the newspaper!"

Grandpa tells Mark who passed away in the last week, jogging Mark's memory about how he knows them. The name doesn't say much to Mark, but to avoid disappointing Grandpa, he pretends to recognize it.

They also talk about the weather, the water levels, and the sturdiness of the dike. And of course, about the large amount of tourists roaming the island. Traditions aren't there for nothing, it turns out.

***

After starting on his second cup of coffee, Grandpa asks about Mark's work. Mark catches him up and tells him about the daily hustle and bustle of his job. He tells a few anecdotes about how things went wrong a few times, but how he was able to save the day with his quick and intelligent thinking.

Most recently, one of the teams had made the decision to install the first version of a new software program. They were trying to solve two problems at the same time: they sought to extinguish a small operational problem, and to connect a supplier who had been nagging for months to the system, so that they could deliver the newest payment terminal.

As always, they had installed the program in the evening, to mitigate some risks, but they only realized that it didn't work when the stores opened and many customers were simultaneously, unsuccessfully trying to pay with their debit cards. They had tried to reset the system back to its old, functional state, but that failed completely. The program was failing to connect to the banks' payment networks, and the result was that customers couldn't pay with their debit cards anymore for 24 hours.

There were long lines at the cash registers of customers who weren't carrying enough cash to pay. Thankfully, at many locations there was at least one bank with an ATM nearby, which allowed customers to get the cash they needed to pay for their items. But still, it was a lot of chaos. The company's Twitter exploded, with complaints pouring in and making it all the way to CNN! And didn't Mark know it. His fellow directors were waiting on the line and the CEO was furious.

Mark certainly learned from that experience. When things go wrong, he's still the head honcho. And how was it possible! The guys in his teams had made an innocent decision in good faith, but Mark would get the entire backlash. Luckily, he was able to fix everything by working through the whole night with one of his managers, so that it was all in order the next day. He did receive compliments relating to the speed with which he solved the problem. But Mark had learned his lesson.

He sees that his Grandfather is trying to understand, but it's still far from his cup of tea. Quite logical, really. Grandpa is a real islander, and therefore he's not exposed to Mark's line of work. Offices, computers, logistical processes: Grandpa is not familiar with it. He used to be a beekeeper, but stopped with that quite early on because it didn't prove to be rewarding. As Mark talks about the current reorganization of the company, thereby switching to the topic of self-managing teams, Grandpa seems genuinely interested. With his utterance of the word 'self-managing' he sees Grandpa look up. "Self-managing? What do you mean by that?"

"Well," answers Mark, "the bottom line is that we are making teams of one to eight people who share equal responsibility."

Grandpa asks: "Fully self-managing? Can they really decide everything themselves?"

"For the most part, yes," says Mark. "The idea is that each team gets the responsibility and therefore must take all the operational decisions. As a team, because there is no direct manager. They organize themselves. Which in itself is not such a bad idea? Usually the team members know the most about the project. So why not let them decide?"

"And you don't intervene at all?" asks Grandpa. Mark gets the impression that he's looking for something.

He replies: "Well, not interfering is tough. Because in many cases, you will see that the teams are not used to taking responsibility. So when it really starts to get tricky and there are problems that clients are confronted with, only then do you notice that they don't know what to do and what they are allowed to decide. In that case I have to jump in, making decisions or helping solve the problem."

"Ah," says Grandpa, "so basically you're secretly still the boss, not the teams. Back in the day we used to call that 'being the boss when the rooster is busy'."

Mark looks surprised. What does Grandpa mean? He replies: "Well, Grandpa, now you have to tell me why that interests you. Now that we're talking about self-managing teams, I suddenly have your full attention."

Grandpa smiles and says: "Yeah, you don't get that huh. Well, I'll explain. But you might want to pour yourself some more coffee, because it's a long story." Grandpa, while rubbing his cold hands together, straightens up in his chair and starts to tell the story.

"Everything played out here on the island, long ago. At that time we only really had agriculture and livestock. Cows, but also a lot of sheep. And I was one of the shepherds. That was long before you were born; your mother hadn't even been born yet. I can imagine that this was never related to you; sheep were very important for us. The wool from our sheep went to the shore, which earned us a pretty penny. Without beating my chest too much, I was perhaps the best shepherd on the island."

He continued: "But I didn't do that work alone. I had a very good dog, and a wonderful flock of sheep."

Grandpa sighs, and there is silence. You can see him think back fondly to that beautiful time. He stares straight ahead, like a shepherd peering into the distance. Mark sees the nostalgic joy in his grandfather, and wants to ask a question. But Grandpa raises his hand, indicating that Mark will have to save his question for later. He picks up the story right where he left off.

"No, I'm not done yet. In fact, this is just the beginning.

One day I was asked to come to the island's council. You know, they gather here once a week in the town hall. The island council was pretty much a platform for discussing the ins and outs of the whole island. We didn't have a real mayor or anything like that, but things still ran pretty smoothly.

Well, the island council gave me a job. The main issue was that we only earned money with our sheep. Mainly the wool, but also the meat of the sheep. Yes, sometimes we had a good potato harvest and we could sell some potatoes. Or apples...

But I digress. It was about money that we could use to improve the island. For example, for the new road, the sewer, the church, or stones alongside the dike. Money is important if you want to buy things on the shore. Now, one of the members of the island council had a brother on another island, abroad. And that brother had written him that they earned quite a bit of money by farming honey. Our island council saw an opportunity there. And they figured that I was the right person for the job. I was namely one of the best shepherds on the island, so if there was someone who could get the job done, it was me. At least, that's what they thought. And I did too. And I felt honored.

Oh, oh, oh, what a drama that was in the beginning. I had no knowledge about bees. One of the village elders, the one with the brother on another island, had given me a book about beekeeping, but that was it. Thick, that book! Well, I looked at the covers of that book and promptly threw it away.

But you might be wondering why I'm telling you this—and especially why I'm telling you this after your remark about teams. Well, look, I have learned that sheep and bees are totally different creatures. In fact, bees manage themselves. Hence my interest when you mentioned self-managing teams. But with sheep, now that was a different story. There, I was the boss. But with the bees, that didn't work at all. And I know they say that 'change is the spice of life,' but in the beginning there was not much to eat, you know!"

Grandpa again falls silent and looks ahead, all the while rubbing his hands together to get warm. Mark is not quite sure what to say. Sheep and bees. How does Grandpa see a connection to his work? Mark's people aren't sheep, after all.

He says, "But Grandpa, didn't you get bees instead of sheep? You don't have to teach bees to make honey, right? That's just what they do. Why would that have anything to do with me?"

"You know what it is," Grandpa replied, "you are absolutely right. I get that things are different for you. Your people aren't sheep or bees. But I did not try to let my sheep gather honey. It therefore seems even more complicated for your people."

He adds: "What it's about for me is the other side. The side of the shepherd. Leading the flock. Bees don't need direction. In nature, without a beekeeper, a bee colony survives just fine. As a beekeeper you have some influence, but it's a totally different type of influence than with sheep. And I wasn't used to that. I was accustomed to my sheep and my flock. It took me quite some time before I realized how it worked, with those bees.

In fact, I had to do it completely differently! What always worked with my sheep didn't work at all with the bees. I myself was the one who had the most to learn, not the bees. I had to teach myself what I would need to do as a beekeeper. That's why I bring it up. Because they always say: 'What Hans doesn't learn, Hans doesn't know'!

I think you should look for your 'beekeeper rules,' as I was back then. You'll have to figure out what's not working and what needs to happen instead. You'll have to find out what to do, what not to worry about, and what you should never forget! And that's not easy. You'll get there through trial and error, as it were. I remember that quite well.

Now that I'm talking about it, I think I still have some notes lying around somewhere from those times. In the beginning I didn't know anything about bees, so I kept a notebook with me. That worked better than that thick theoretic book. Eventually, I got it down and it wasn't a thing. For a while, at least."

Mark sees Grandpa's restrained facial expression, and asks cheekily: "What do you mean, for a while?"

Grandpa answers: "Well, it went quite well. Until…hey, wait a minute. I have an idea. Why don't you go biking or whatever, and in the meantime I'll dig up that notebook. Come back this afternoon around half past three for a cup of tea. Then we can look at it together. Then you can see if it's of any use to you. Aunt Ronda always makes me take an afternoon nap, but today I'll just look for that notebook in the attic instead. Sound good?"

Well, you can see where Aunt Ronda got her commanding nature from, Mark ponders with a smile. He replies: "Fine, Grandpa, I'll come by this afternoon for some tea. Mornings and evenings I drink strong coffee, but in the afternoon I love a cup of tea."

When Mark gets up and walks towards the back door, he hears his Grandpa climbing the stairs. He hears him mutter about the notebook. Mark calls after him: "Oh yeah, Grandpa, don't forget to take those red pills!" But it is not clear whether Grandpa heard him or not.

***

During the rest of the morning, Mark goes for a lovely ride on his mountain bike. While he's biking, he has plenty of time to put his thoughts in order. Does Grandpa have a point? Is the change in Mark himself? And is it really not that much harder for Mark and his teams? Grandpa got new bees instead of sheep. The bees knew exactly what to do. In Mark's situation, his people will have to start behaving rather differently: by taking responsibility, managing themselves, and correcting each other. Yet that was precisely not the intention. Mark seems to be asking his people, the same people, to behave drastically differently. Is that fair? Doesn't that make their lives more difficult? Doesn't that make it much more likely that they will just fall back on what they have always done?

He has a hunch. Yes, for his people it will be more difficult, because they have to change their behavior. On the other hand, people are much more flexible and intelligent than bees or sheep, so it doesn't have to be so difficult. His hunch now circles back to Mark himself. If he does not change himself, his people can't exactly be expected to blossom! Does Mark hold the key to figuring this out? If he doesn't do things differently, he would be like a shepherd trying to keep a swarm of bees in line. That approach is, of course, doomed to fail.

While he's biking, he realizes that he has a lot to discover himself as well. And he recognizes that any rookie management mistake that he makes would just be seen by his people as confirmation that they don't have to be self-managing. Indeed, Mark remains the great problem solver.

Mark understands that he needs to look for new ways, a sort of new rulebook. Rules for himself. What did Grandpa call that again? Oh yes, his beekeeper rules. How do you lead self-managing teams? How do you keep control? When are you supposed to do nothing, even when everything inside you screams at you to intervene? And conversely, when must you intervene, despite having the feeling that the teams should be able to figure it out themselves? And how do you intervene? Rendering operational assistance doesn't exactly help make a team self-managing. So how exactly does that work?

What does this new form of leadership look like? Mark ponders it while pushing the bike along. He realizes that he doesn't understand the new rules of the game. Additionally, he has recently committed to contribute to the new training program for managers and business leaders. It might be a nice idea to discuss leading self-managing teams, and how to do it in practice. Let's see if I can make the presentation during this vacation, he thinks to himself. I can listen to more of Grandpa's anecdotes, which would immediately give me some great analogies for the presentation.

Then his thoughts turn to Susan. If he's being honest, he can't be mad at her for sacrificing their short vacation due to circumstances at work. How many evenings and weekends engagements has he cancelled at the last minute? Mark sighs. There has to be another way.

***

Along the way, he has lunch and then promptly returns to Aunt Ronda's house. The salty sea breeze and the physical exertion from the bike ride are great, but they make him tired. But hey, he's on vacation. So why not?

3. Shearing Bees

It's half past three when Mark steps into Grandpa's house. Grandpa is already at the table. Mark spots some cobwebs in his wavy ponytail and smiles. A large teapot with steaming hot tea is positioned in the center of the table. It's impressive that he's still so on top of things, despite his age. He's considerably into his nineties, actually. Yes, Aunt Ronda extends a helping hand every now and then and lives near him. And yes, it is sometimes a bit of a mess in his house with all those old newspapers scattered around, but all in all it's still pretty clean. In terms of Grandpa's clothing, it's always a hodgepodge; a mix and match type thing. He does faithfully wear a shirt, covered by a sweater, but somehow he always succeeds in wearing two different colors that don't match at all.

Grandpa smiles welcomingly toward him: "Hey Junior, sit down! I found my notebook. Say, I hadn't been in the attic for a while. What a dusty mess it is up there. "A bad coughing bout immediately follows his comment. A quick sip of tea all but eliminates his coughing.

"I found even more junk up there. I even found a whole collection of slides and a projector! I didn't know I had those lying around. I actually spent most the time after you left in the attic just now. Don't tell Aunt Ronda, okay?" He adds immediately. "She always gets so worried if I skip my afternoon nap. And she's always whining about those pills! Speaking of which, I think I forgot to take those this morning. Well, better do it now."

He searches underneath the stack of newspapers for his pill box, eventually finding it and removing two large red pills. "Just like Skittles, but for my ticker!" He swallows the pills with a swig of tea, and coughs again.

"Look, here's the notebook!" He shouts, as he triumphantly displays a rugged, worn out school notebook. It's true the book survived its time in the attic, but you can see by the damage that it's been heavily used.

"It took me a while to find, but it was in a box along with my beekeeper suit. I've been thumbing through it already, and I came across something I totally forgot about."

"Oh yeah? What was it?" Marks asks, clearly intrigued.

"Well," Grandpa replies, "I completely forgot that my biggest mistake was waiting until the end. Waiting until the end of the Fall."

Mark doesn't quite understand: "What do you mean?"

Grandpa answers him: "Look, I sheared my sheep as late as possible. The quantity of wool and the thickness of the coat determined the yield. So I always waited as long as possible.

I did so with my bees, too. And you know, bees are very different for that matter. If you wait until the end, then their beehive fills up and they stop. It is their job to prepare the swarm for the winter. Once they've prepared sufficiently, they stop producing. After they stop, the overwhelming majority of the bees die. Most people don't know this, but each year 85% of the swarm dies. Essentially, if I waited until the end, then I would get less honey since the bees had started dying.

It took quite a while before I realized that you need to 'shear' the bees in the meantime, if you get what I mean. You should periodically remove the full combs. Only when the honey disappears from the hive do the bees start producing more honey. Bees will naturally continue making honey as long as there is room in the hive to store it. And if they run out of room, then you have to free up some space. Otherwise, they stop.

I don't know why I'm telling you this, but it was one of the things I learned the hard way. And I almost forgot about it, too! Do you recognize any of this, or am I just rambling on?"

Mark thinks for a moment and replies: "Yes, I recognize it. You can recognize that in many different businesses. For example, the end of the month closure. Good or bad does not matter: the counters go back to zero and everyone gets a fresh start. It's like that at my job, too. But if I'm honest, we wait longer in many different situations. We have big projects that we incorporate into even larger projects, and because we want to be as streamlined and efficient as possible, we plan it so that everything is only done at the end. Unfortunately it does not work out too well, and drags on over time. Usually, such projects are a total mess, and nothing positive comes out of them!"

He continues: "In addition, we also need to make an incentive structure. That seems the most like 'shearing' to me. That too we don't do until the end. We only evaluate performance and give out bonuses at the end of the year. Then we 'shear' our people. You could say that people sometimes stop before it's time too, just like bees, but they stop with their personal development instead of honey.

Now that I say it like that, maybe that is one of the causes. The longer we delay the fruits of the labor, the greater the chance of failure!"

"Well," Grandpa responds, "With regard to scale, I recognize that for sure. Once I made a huge bee hive. Just massive. As a shepherd, having one large herd is better than having several small ones. You can't be everywhere at once, after all. So I thought, just like with my sheep: the bigger the hive, the more bees, and thus the more honey. But that's not how it works, unfortunately.

When I tried to harvest the honey in the bee hive at the end of that season, it was a complete failure. Why? A colony does not like a large hive. In fact, they don't have the 'manpower' to fill the whole hive. So that colony would abandon the cabinet and build a new hive somewhere else. If I had harvested more honey, I would have learned much sooner that an oversized hive doesn't work."

Grandpa continues: "I had to discover that it actually helps the bees to remove the honey from the hive. As a beekeeper, you take the full trays out of the cabinet and put in empty ones. Then the bees have something to do. And as long as there are enough blooming flowers, they will keep at it. This results in much more honey production. And it gave me the ability to taste the honey earlier on in the process. After all, they don't say 'If you don't taste the pudding, then it's not for eating,' for no reason!"

"That's useful for me," said Mark. "My people are inspired by success. They get happy when they see things working and when clients are happy with their work product. Honestly, we don't celebrate these successes enough. The act of harvesting honey can be seen as celebrating success. The more, the better!"

"Well, be careful!" Exclaimed Grandpa. "Yes, harvesting more frequently than just at the end is fine. But make sure it's not happening too frequently, either! I had to really figure out how often I could take out honey. When I had lots of cabinets at one point, I just got into a certain rhythm."

"Huh," said Mark, "I've heard about that 'rhythm' before. In our company, we have a coach roaming around who always tells me about it. He even proposed that the entire management team work at the same rhythm. Then every week would look the same in terms of meetings. But that really wouldn't work for us. You can't exactly plan out when problems occur. He's a bit of a smart-alec, that guy. He keeps saying that he's done it with all these other companies, that I'll only understand it when I see it in action and then I will have anticipated those problems. His favorite saying is: 'Continuous improvement is more important than delayed perfection.' What a character!"

Grandpa is silent. He stares straight ahead and says: "Yes, I know all about smart-asses. We also had one: William. But that's not who we're talking about right now. Your guy has a point, though. You definitely shouldn't procrastinate until the last moment. Honey must be harvested very frequently! And it had another advantage for me as well. Do you know what?"

"Well, what?" Mark asks curiously.

"That honey harvesting is a real pain. The bees are not fond of it and you have to really choose the right moment. Hence, the beekeeper smokes a special kind of pipe, a 'smoker.' Using the pipe, you blow smoke in the hive body, which calms the bees down. Then they are as meek as a lamb. "

Grandpa smiles as if he realizes that he's unconsciously compared bees with sheep. He continues: "But the important thing is: the more you harvest, the better you get at beekeeping. Ultimately, it comes down to the honey. Harvesting often made for quick improvements to my honey gathering technique!"

"That also sounds familiar," Mark says enthusiastically. "With us, we have the tendency to push things back until it's perfect. That's not too bad in principle, because what's wrong with quality? At the same time, you do not push to deliver quickly and frequently. You have the tendency to procrastinate and thus accomplish less. For example, it took us three years before customers could order groceries via our website for home delivery. That was unacceptable."

"I recognize that," replies Grandpa. "Customers don't expect to wait; they will just buy their honey elsewhere."

**

They're still in the middle of their conversation when Aunt Ronda comes in with two piping hot, steaming pans. She immediately begins to clean the empty table. The cups and teapot disappear directly into the kitchen.

"Pass that old teapot under the newspapers over here," she requests of Grandpa.

"No, you're not getting that one," he replies. "That's lemon tea. I'll drink it tonight after dinner. Lemon tea tastes much better when it has cooled down!"

Meanwhile, Mark helps set the table. They eat a potato-carrot mash with meatballs on the side. It's not incredibly tasty; Aunt Ronda doesn't season the food with salt when she cooks for Grandpa. Mark hadn't thought of that. Don't forget to buy some salt tomorrow, he reminded himself.

Right as they finished eating, Mark's phone rings. It's Susan. She's no longer making remarks about the fact that Mark went on vacation by himself. Apparently, the worst of her anger has now subsided. Mark walks outside to speak to her privately. He tells her about the island and about how things are going with Grandpa and Aunt Ronda.

The reason for Susan's calls happens to be Mandy, their daughter. She's a lovely, cheerful girl who gives off a vibe of wanting to tackle the world. She's in her sophomore year of High School and is making good academic progress, but she just doesn't like it. It's too theoretical, she says. She would rather be doing things than sitting at her desk, which she finds unexciting. Luckily, she has a part time job on Friday afternoon and Saturday, in the local hospital. She loves her job there; and it turns out that's what Susan is calling about. Mandy has been invited to join the hospital's occupational nurse training program, which she could do in conjunction with her regular job. And that is totally her thing; she's very enthusiastic about it. Susan supports her in it. "Follow your heart and your passion, then you will always find your target" is one of her trademark sayings.

Mark is not as thrilled and disagrees with her. Mandy has only two more years of High School left before she gets her diploma, after which she could always go into patient care if she wanted to. She would also have the option to go to college and become a Doctor. "Diplomas are for life!" He hears himself saying to Susan. "I don't think that's a good idea. Can't she just finish High School first? Why stop now before getting the degree? Maybe this will turn out to be a fad!"

He hears Mandy's heated tone of voice in the background. Apparently she's also listening. "To hell with Dad's objections!" She shouts fiercely. "I'll do it anyway. Whether he likes it or not!"

Susan tries to calm things down. Eventually, she says: "Mark, sleep on it for a night. If Mandy wants to follow her passion, she will discover for herself whether it's a good choice or not."

Mark replies, clearly annoyed: "We're not going to let Mandy throw away her future like that, are we? Why are you encouraging her to do this? Just two more years in High School and then she can go straight to college!"

They remain unconvinced. Mark hangs up the phone angrily. This is already the second time this week that they are arguing.

After that difficult call, Mark goes back into Grandpa's house. Aunt Ronda has put the dirty dishes in a tub, ready to be taken away. They walk to her house together and do the dishes. By hand, of course.

Grandpa already looked pretty tired when they left him, and he promised not to go to bed too late. He had skipped his afternoon nap, after all. When Mark and Aunt Ronda walked outside, he had grabbed the teapot from underneath the newspapers to pour himself a cold cup of lemon tea. After that, he would go to bed.

When Mark returns to his room after finishing his share of dishwashing, he picks up his iPad. He opens a new presentation entitled: "How to lead self-managing teams?"

In only fifteen minutes, he summed up the lessons from today. The first page looks like this:

Lesson 1: Harvesting Frequently Gets Results

- **Usable results are the only measure of progress**
  Customers can only get utility from conclusive, usable results. So always be results-oriented. Pushing the results back works against you; you see no progress in the interim, and you learn way too late what does and doesn't work and what has value.
- **Delivering frequently and regularly is crucial**
  Deliver often, this always makes customers happy. And as an added bonus, you also get better at it since you do it more often. Making customers happy is its own kind of encouragement and stimulation. The more you can deliver results and observe them, the sooner you can test quality and the more appreciation and motivation you feel.
- **Do not delay acknowledgement of good work**
  Rewarding and complimenting people helps them to shine. If you do it too late, then it's not motivating your people do better work. That is a shame.
- **A steady rhythm helps**
  Rhythm brings synchronization and gives structure. With a steady rhythm, it is always clear when the next result can be expected. Then the counter goes back to zero, and everyone can make a fresh start. Working within a rhythm and delivering usable results is always sufficient.

Mark listens to his voicemails and begins answering some emails. He notices that there are many references to operational things in his correspondence. Three voicemails regarding the new self-scanners and the related technical decisions that have to be made as a consequence. Self-management seems quite a ways off, he thought to himself. He drafts a long email for the project team in which he indicates what they need to do and which interfaces need to be adjusted.

    Afterwards, he sends a text message to Susan: *"Sorry about earlier. I just think it's very unwise. Please think about it carefully! Call you tomorrow xxx"*

4. Lex

The next morning Mark tries to sleep in, but it just doesn't work. He's already up and thinking about the situation with Mandy. He also knows that she's really enjoying working at the hospital. In a sense, that occupational training could be a good fit for her; she is a doer after all. But all those years of High School would be wasted. She is quite good at learning and is smart enough to attend a college and maybe become a Doctor one day. Those last two years of High School would give her a diploma and a certain path for the future. After that, she could always decide to be a nurse.

He is most disappointed in Susan. Mark gets the impression that the decision has already been made behind his back. That's the type of thing that you would decide on together, he thought. He tries to go back to sleep a little bit, but ends up tossing and turning without succeeding.

***

Still, it's only half past nine when he walks into Aunt Ronda's kitchen. Surprised, she looks up. "What? Did you only just get out of bed?" she asks. "I thought you were such an early bird?"

Mark replies: "Normally speaking I am, but this time I wasn't able to sleep well. Lots to think about at work." He doesn't clue her in on the situation with Mandy; Aunt Ronda is indeed rather nosy. He could totally see her calling Susan and Mandy to discuss the matter.

She shakes her head. "Poor guy. What are you doing? You're on vacation and all you're thinking about is your work. That doesn't seem right. That's not why they call it vacation, is it?"

She continues: "If you can't sleep well next time, just say so. Then I'll make you a cup of fennel tea. I always take a cup before going to bed myself."

"Aunt Ronda, you're a sweetheart," Mark replied. "Next time, I definitely will ask. Can I make a quick breakfast for myself?"

"No way," she says. "You go take a shower, and I'll make breakfast for you in the meantime. Then I'll have my way!" She laughs. "By the way, do you have any plans for today?"

"Yeah," Mark says, nodding. "I think I'm going to go for a scenic car ride with Grandpa. The sun is shining, so I think it will be some good riding!"

"Be careful now," she responds immediately. "Yesterday he was already coughing. Especially in the afternoon. He's about at that age...he develops a cough rather easily. So make sure the roof is closed on that strange car of yours, okay? A car without a roof is enough of a threat. Otherwise Grandpa will get sick!"

"Oh I know," Mark answered. "No problem. The top will remain shut. Maybe that's better for Grandpa anyway, considering the warm weather. We'll just turn the AC on, then it won't be too hot for him!"

Before Aunt Ronda even had the chance to mention that having the AC on could be just as bad, Mark ran up the stairs. He's starting to understand what Grandpa means when he refers to her nosiness.

***

Grandpa is delighted with the idea. Later in the afternoon, and with several stiff movements, Grandpa gets into Mark's car. He brought his old sheepherder's staff in the car: a long stick with the characteristic curve at the end.

Grandpa is not quite as mobile and uses the staff as a walking stick. And it's kind of an operation to get the darn thing in Mark's car.

Aunt Ronda had demanded that they would leave only after Grandpa's afternoon nap. Moreover, she insisted that he wear a scarf in the car, because she's always scared that it will be too cold. She walks up with a canary yellow scarf. From her choice of color, Mark realizes that she inherited her fashion style from her dad. Grandpa's sweater and undershirt already don't match, but with the yellow scarf the combination looks even more risqué. Grandpa argues back, saying that she must be crazy to send him off on such a nice day with such a hefty scarf. But eventually, he relents. He was probably afraid that he wouldn't be able to leave otherwise.

Now they were on their way, zipping around the island with the top down. Grandpa insisted. "Have you gone completely mad?" he had grumbled, "In this kind of weather, you drive with the top down! Is that 'concern-virus' contagious or something? Ronda has it and now you have it too? Open that thing! I want to sit in the sun!" He did urge Mark to only drop the top once they were out of sight, so he did care about appearances.

And so it was happening. Grandpa's long, gray hair flagellated in all different directions.

They made a wonderful trip around the island. Mark didn't remember the route too well, but Grandpa did. He knows every path and road. Most of them are unfortunately not accessible by car, but nevertheless they arrived at kinds of places on the island that Mark couldn't remember or recognize. He begins to understand why. Grandpa has always wandered the island with his flock of sheep, and after that his beehives were spread all over the island. When they all have tea together that afternoon at a local café, Mark reflects on the great day they had.

"Say, Grandpa, I've been thinking. What you were saying about bees and self-management, that's not really true, is it? I have always understood that there is a highly specialized division of labor in a colony of bees. And there's only one Queen, of course."

Grandpa seems embarrassed with the question, and answers: "You know, on the one hand you are right. A colony needs a meticulous division of labor. Indeed, there's only one Queen, but be careful; she's not actually the boss! The Queen lays eggs and thereby provides for the long term longevity of the colony. That is why she's the Queen; it has nothing to do with being in charge. And what's also special is that the colony chooses its Queen. As a beekeeper you have absolutely no influence in that process. It was different when I was a sheepherder, where I decided which rams could be with the sheep. I decided everything."

"But Grandpa," Mark responds, "is there really nobody in charge in the flock? Is it really the sheepherder? Is there not a sheep that leads the flock? As the saying goes, 'once the first sheep crosses the dike, the rest follow.' That implies that there is a leader among them."

"Ha, ha, oh Mark," Grandpa says laughingly, "you don't know much about sheep, do you? No, sheep just follow the sheep walking directly in front of them. It doesn't matter which sheep it is. But now that we're talking about it, there was one in my flock that took on a leading role. That was Lex!"

"Lex?"

"Yes, Lex. My dog! All of the sheep listened to Lex. He could lead them. What a magnificent dog he was. I still carry a photo of him in my wallet. Look!"

Grandpa rummages around in his pocket to grab his wallet, and presents Mark with a crumpled black and white photo of himself and a border collie. A real typical sheepherder's dog. Grandpa stands alongside him proudly. Long locks of blonde hair drape over his shoulders.

In the background, Mark makes out a large flock of sheep and the silhouette of a sheepherder's staff. It's precisely the same staff Grandpa used on his walk earlier that day.

"Lex really was the best. He had a good sense of awareness, and knew exactly how to drive the sheep and keep the flock tight. Wonderful! A single bark was enough to spur the sheep into action; they really revered him.

But he protected the sheep as well. We once had two stray dogs wreaking havoc on the island. They tried to attack the sheep and eat them. But with Lex on watch, they weren't able to catch a single one. He barked and bit, whatever he needed to do. The next day, there were three sheep with blood stains on their coat, but it wasn't sheep blood. Lex had fought for his own life, and for the life of the sheep in his flock!

So indeed, the sheep were essentially led, namely by Lex. And I was Lex's boss, of course. A very clear hierarchy."

Mark ponders and reacts: "Hmm, yes, barking dogs. We've got a couple of those back at the office too. They too can bark; we call them managers!" He laughs. "Project Managers, Marketing Managers, Team Managers, Department Managers, HR Managers, and so on. The one barks louder than the other, but bark they certainly do. And some even bite! There are definitely a couple that could be compared with Lex. The way they work with others really resembles driving a herd of sheep!

What did you do with Lex by the way, Grandpa, when you started beekeeping? And what happened to your sheep?"

Grandpa replies: "My sheep got a new herder, which was arranged by the island council. But Lex, I kept. I wanted to keep him; he was my dog and it really felt that way. I couldn't let him go, so I kept him."

Grandpa closes his eyes and sighs deeply. "Yeah, that was quite something in the beginning. Of course, it was a total disaster. Not that I was so naive that I tried to lead a colony of bees with Lex; I wasn't that dumb. But I did bring Lex with me when I visited the bees."

"And did that work, Grandpa?"

"No it didn't son, it was a complete failure. Lex was all wound up. Everything that he did with the sheep, the bees did independently. Lex would always help to drive the flock, but the bees did that themselves. And at night, Lex would keep a watch, which was also not necessary for the bee colony. A bee sting is often much more painful than a dog bite anyway. As the saying goes, 'The little bee, light and small, packs a punch after all.'

In the beginning I did take Lex to the bee cabinets, but the barking was quite counterproductive. The bees hated it; it made them nervous, which in turn was not good for the honey. No, barking didn't work with bees. You have to leave them alone...so definitely no barking!

Lex and the bees eventually had a good synergy, though. I still remember when Lex snatched one out of the air once. He jumped up and snatched him with one fell swoop. But then the damn bee stung his tongue! Lex, after writhing temporarily, ran off and disappeared for the rest of the day!

Another time, he even jumped against the bee cabinets. In a split second, half of the colony started going after him. That truly was dangerous. Thankfully, he was faster and was able to jump into a nearby creek, otherwise I don't know how that would've played out.

After that, I let him go back home. And do you know what was the scariest of all?"

"No idea, what was it?" Mark counters.

"Well, at a certain point, it wasn't Lex anymore. He was so good in his work with the sheep. That was his pride and joy, and he got restless when he didn't have anything to do anymore. It was just sad to see. I actually thought he was sick for a while. In the mornings he would always stay in his cot, and it seemed like the life had been sucked out of him. In the end, I decided to put an end to it; he just wasn't himself anymore."

"Did you give him a shot?" Mark asks, clearly somewhat surprised and shocked.

"Of course not, boy!" Grandpa retorts in his booming voice. "What do you think? No, I gave him away. To the herder who took over my flock, actually. He already had a dog, but he said he could use a second one. He was so happy with Lex. And Lex maybe with him as well! I went to visit him one time and he seemed completely in his element."

"And how did you find that, then? You decided, just like Lex, exactly what happened. So how was it to not have to lead? That the bees led themselves?"

Grandpa sits in thought, staring off into the distance, as if he's looking over the fields. Then he answers: "In the beginning, that took some getting used to. My leadership over the flock was precisely what made me one of the best shepherds on the island. I had to un-learn that. I vividly remember the first week that I had the bees. I sat near the cabinets. At a distance, of course, but I did stay close by. It was torturous! You see the bees flying, but you have no idea what they're doing. And it's not like you can just stop by every hour and hurry them along, because then they get agitated and stop producing honey at all. Or they sting you. Letting go was the key. I had to trust that a strong work ethic was in their nature, and that they had it all under control. Not only that I could leave them to do their thing, but that I should leave them alone for the best outcome. And do you know what the big advantage is of that, Mark?"

Mark shakes his head.

"That empowers you to do much more. With the sheep, I could only have one flock at a time. With Lex at my side, a larger flock than I could handle by myself of course, but still only one flock. Because I had to make every decision and direct the flock, I always had to be present."

"What do you mean?" asks Mark. "I don't think I understand."

Grandpa explains: "As a beekeeper you can handle many cabinets. Every colony has its own cabinet, so therefore you can manage many colonies. And each colony leads itself. You can be gone for quite a while and don't need to always be sitting right on top of things. The extent to which the island's flowers blossom determines how many colonies you can keep. It has nothing to do with the beekeeper. The amount of wool depends on the number of sheep, which was determined by Lex and me. Not by the sheep or by the quantity of land available for grazing.

Since the bees arranged everything themselves, I only had to make sure that the honey was collected promptly, and that didn't take long so theoretically I could have 150 cabinets on this island. 150! With the sheep, it was unthinkable to have more than one flock, let alone 150!

I only needed to decide where, and how many, cabinets needed to be placed and that was it."

Mark thinks about all of the self-managing teams that are going to be working under him. He wonders for a second if he might have less of a need for managers than before. He asks: "Is that really it? The location of the cabinet, the quantity, and collecting the honey?"

"Yep, that's the gist of it," Grandpa replies. "There were a couple more things, of course, but then I would need to get my journal. But that is the most important thing: positioning the cabinets and their colonies strategically, so that they have a goal, and then collecting the honey as they produce! The bees take care of the rest."

"I can't imagine that it could be so simple for us, Grandpa," says Mark. "I have to think about it more, because it seems a touch too simple."

"Hold on boy," Grandpa responds, "it is not simple at all! It's actually quite difficult. There's a lot more to pay attention to, and you have to look beyond the work itself. But I'll explain that another time. You go ponder some more about the barking and biting. And don't forget to think about that in the context of your leadership, too!"

Mark looks at him with a confused gaze. "How do you mean?"

"Well, I did notice that you named your managers when we were talking about barking, but you didn't include yourself. I don't know, but when I was leading Lex, it meant that I had trained him to work a certain way. Lex listened to me astutely. How have you trained your managers? How often do you walk around barking? Every moment that you play the boss and give directives, you are barking! You might not recognize it as barking yourself, but it wouldn't surprise me if that's what you do all day. I heard you speak with Susan last night, now that also sounded like barking. We could hear you inside!". Grandpa adds: "Mark, you might be more like Lex than you think! And that nobody would tell you that doesn't surprise me at all."

Mark is shocked by Grandpa's frankness; he has never spoken to him this way before. But he does feel that Grandpa is getting at something, and he's sensitive to that. Mark was indeed rather quick to name his managers without mentioning himself, notwithstanding his conversation with Susan. Do his people only listen to him because he has power? Is he really the inspirational leader that he needs to be? Is his passion for solving problems indicative of that fact that he still has a lot to work on himself? Is he also barking back at home to keep things moving?

***

On the way home, it's rather quiet in the car. Mark is reflecting introspectively, and Grandpa is tired. He even falls asleep in the car, mid-sentence. Mark was worried for a second, but then calmed down after he heard Grandpa's characteristic snore. One little strand of Grandpa's long, gray hair hangs in front of his face, and with every snore it flagellates rhythmically. It looks somewhat comedic. It was a nice day of exploring together, Mark thought to himself; the wind at their backs and faces in the sun. It's not surprising that Grandpa was tired.

When they arrive back home, Grandpa wakes up. He invites Mark inside for a cup of cold lemon tea. Mark thanks him for the invitation, but reminds him that he has to help Aunt Ronda with cooking. That would also give him a chance to freshen up and ensure that there was at least a little bit of salt in his portion.

They all ate together. After washing the dishes, Mark tries to call Susan a couple of times, but he gets her voicemail. Mandy isn't picking up either. Mark decides to grab his iPad and make a summary of what he remembered from the day. He whips up a second lesson sheet with the big points.

Lesson 2: Disrupting Operational Direction

- **Trust the teams.**
  A self-managing team of experts knows what is best, and even when they don't it provides a learning opportunity. Don't doubt your team's competence and always be trusting.
- **Make it clear what the goal is.**
  The only thing that counts is the value and the magnitude of the final product. Give them a goal, make the result transparent, and let the teams fill in the rest.
- **Stop micromanaging, and don't bark**
  Trust that it is in your team's nature to be as efficient and effective as possible. Don't exercise your authority. Make sure that your teams know how to handle special situations. If you need to lead by exerting your power, it's a sign that you're too late.
- **Make yourself superfluous**
  Set goals for your teams and let them make the decisions to get there. At the point where they need to start making decisions rapidly, make it abundantly clear what the team can decide and what will be decided upon later. Make sure that you are not needed for that.

When he's finished, it's already 9 PM. Mark considers stopping by to see Grandpa again, but he decides against it. It was an exhausting day, running around the island, and if he slept soon it would be by a reasonable hour. But first, he goes through his entire inbox, firing off myriad emails to decide on some action items for the team to implement. He dreams that night about nursing degrees that you can just buy at the supermarket.

5. Cabinets and Frameworks

Mark is already out and about first thing the next morning, mountain biking along some of the island's scenic paths. It's a lovely day, and he bikes through the dunes and goes back via the beach. He's the only one on the dunes, but when he gets to the ocean he's no longer alone. A group of hikers trudges along and several dogs play on the beach, with their owners looking on amusedly.

Tired but satisfied, Mark eats breakfast in the old town hall and reads the newspaper. He feels at ease there. He often thinks about the impact that this place has had on his Grandpa. It all started here. This is where Grandpa was asked, due to his success in sheepherding, to also keep the island's bees.

The more Mark thinks about it, the stranger it becomes. Why would you take someone who's so successful at their trade and take them away from it? You would be losing your best shepherd! It's a waste of Grandpa's talents, really.

Mark also gets to have a brief chat with Susan. She doesn't have much time since things are really busy at work. She will call him later at night. She wasn't able to talk last night because she went with Mandy to an information session for aspiring nurses. Mark is surprised and gets a few words in, but then they are disconnected. She's back to work.

***

When Mark stops by his Grandpa's place that morning, he has a question ready: "Grandpa, I've been thinking. Isn't it somewhat illogical to ask your best shepherd to become a beekeeper?"

Grandpa, who was still buried deep in the newspaper, looks up at once and replies: "Well, when you put it that way…I have thought about that before, but I think the island council just didn't want to take any risks. Nobody had experience with bees, you see. Keep that in mind. We were doing something completely new, without any relevant knowledge or experience. Those are the kinds of tasks you want your best people working on. We had no idea what was going to happen and how it would go. What do you do in those instances?"

Mark thinks for a second. "Well, you've got a point. A while back I had something very novel at my fingertips. A brand new technology that, if it performed as promised, would signify a huge breakthrough. To find out if it would work as planned and could live up to its promise, I started a project. And indeed, I put two of my best people on it. If it wouldn't work even then, then I at least knew that it was something with the technology getting in the way; it wasn't our approach or the people."

"Exactly," Grandpa answers. "Our Island Council must have thought roughly the same. If we're going to be trying something completely new, let's have it be led by someone capable enough to maintain oversight and control. That's probably why they asked me. I was good with the sheep, wasn't afraid of anything, and was willing to try new things. It went pretty well too, until that idiot William came along."

That's the second time that Grandpa mentions William. Mark wants to know the story there and asks: "William? Who is William again, Grandpa?"

At that moment, Aunt Ronda enters the room. She had just heard Mark's question and reacts directly: "What? Are you guys talking about William? Dad, I don't want you to talk with Mark about William. You know what it does to you; and you know what the Doctor said!" Her tone of voice is decisive and firm.

"Yeah, yeah, Ronda," Grandpa replies, "I can't get too wound up." At that point, he refocuses his gaze on the ceiling. "Doctors...pffff! Back in the day we didn't even have a Doctor on the island and even then everyone lived past 80."

Aunt Ronda says concernedly: "Dad, take it seriously please. You need to take care of yourself! Did you take your pills already?" She starts to rummage through the newspapers in search of his pillbox. The first thing she grasps is a teapot. She puts her hands around it and feels that the warmth has left it entirely. "And why is there cold tea here? I'm going to take that away and empty it!"

That's when her meddling becomes too much to handle for Grandpa. "Ronda! Stop it!" He commands. "This is my house, and these are my things. I will empty the teapot myself. I don't need you for that. Go away! And I've already taken my pills, so don't worry about it!"

Slightly shocked, she processes for a moment. She wants to walk away, but instead remains pondering. With one hand on her hip and another pointing towards Mark, she reacts. "Mark, one thing. I don't want you to talk about William with Grandpa. Period. It's not good for his blood pressure. You don't know what you're getting yourself into and it doesn't matter anyway. The past is the past. That's enough!"

She makes a beeline for the door, leaving behind an uneasy silence.

***

Grandpa breaks the silence. "Don't worry about her, Mark. This happens about once a week. Ronda is a darling, but she treats everyone like a child. But yeah, she has some points. I shouldn't get too wound up. I love telling stories from the past, so let's just keep it at that. William isn't important anyway. I didn't like him. Never did, never will. And Ronda is right, when I talk about him, I always get angry. Coffee?"

They drink their morning coffee and discuss how busy it is on the island, the weather, the dike, and the rowing advertisements in the newspaper. They arrange to go for a walk to the city hall after Grandpa's afternoon nap. Mark stands up, waves farewell, and heads back to Aunt Ronda's house. When Mark arrives, she's in the kitchen and is waiting for Mark with both hands on her hips.

"Mark, will you have a seat?" she says.

Mark takes his place at the kitchen table, preparing himself for the onslaught.

But it's not too bad in the end. Aunt Ronda sits on the chair next to Mark and says: "Sorry that I let myself go last night. I sometimes worry about your Grandpa and then I think about it too much and he gets all wound up. And that's precisely what I don't want.

Look, my dad is already old. He doesn't get those pills for no reason. The Doctor says he needs to take it easy. He doesn't need to live like a potted plant; doing fun things is all well and good. Like yesterday, going for a little road trip is no problem. But he really can't let himself get wound up. And when he talks about William, he always gets so angry.

Can you avoid bringing up William? It's bad for his health. And that's your responsibility, too. Can you please do that?"

"Of course, Aunt," Mark sympathetically responds. "Believe me, I also want the best for Grandpa. I won't start on the topic again if it winds him up so much. I promise."

Mark makes a peace-sign gesture signifying his promise and stands up. Aunt Ronda looks at him with a concerned look. Mark sees how she worries about her father and throws his arm around her. "Don't worry about it, Aunt Ronda. It will all be okay. Grandpa is stronger than you think and he's fairly fit for his age."

"Yeah yeah, I know," she says. She then looks at Mark and her expression goes sour: "But man, you smell like you haven't showered at all! You stink like sweat, it's nasty! Come on, go upstairs and rinse off!"

Mark laughs. She's right. He went out to breakfast after mountain biking and then went straight to Grandpa's for coffee. He laughs as he ascends the stairway. It's like he's living at home with his mother again.

***

That afternoon, Mark and Grandpa walk to the city hall together. It's a ten minute stroll and Grandpa can handle that fine. He supports himself with his shepherd's staff as he walks. Nobody has one of those, but somehow he doesn't look strange carrying it. Mark can't imagine Grandpa walking through town with a walker. The shepherd's staff is a good alternative for now.

Grandpa orders a normal tea and Mark a fresh mint tea. After five minutes or so, the server brings two steaming cups of tea. She warns that they are very hot.

Grandpa stares at Mark's tea glass skeptically from across the table. "Do you call that tea, Mark? Those mint stems? What you have sitting in your water there, I used to feed to my sheep!"

Mark laughs. "Yeah Grandpa, these modern times, huh. And that's not even the half of it. Your tea is flown in from the other side of the world. Mine, they pick out of the garden in the back. And still my cup of tea is twice as expensive as yours."

Grandpa shakes his head. "It's unbelievable. It can't get crazier than that. I hope you enjoy that taste of grass," he says laughing. "You know what, stay over tonight after dinner. Then I'll give you a cup of ice tea, now that's worth it!" He winks at Mark.

"Sounds good Grandpa," says Mark. "But I do also want to talk about your bees again. I've been thinking more about self-management. I understand that it works with bees making honey, that I get. But it just seems unnatural for me to let people loose without any direction. Like the French say, 'laissez-faire,' but I don't want to use that as a model!"

"I can appreciate that," Grandpa replies. "Doing nothing isn't good either. That I completely agree with. Maybe you will appreciate this next example."

"You see," continues Grandpa, "what was important for my bees was the size of the cabinet. I really had to discover that by trying out many arrangements. You have to give the bees a certain amount of living space in the cabinet. Not too little, but also not too much. And you have to make sure that they work within that space.

A new colony that has branched off should start in a smaller cabinet. When they split up, it's already the middle of the season. And at that point, a huge cabinet is not going to help. So you provide a smaller cabinet to start, and then you relocate the bees to a bigger cabinet later on.

Essentially, you play with the amount of space that they get. Does that help at all?"

Mark ponders. The word 'space' does trigger something within him. "Maybe, Grandpa. We also give our teams a certain amount of space to work, and that is quite comparable. We call it a framework. Frameworks in which they have autonomy and can do their thing. Now that I think about it, it's actually a little strange that all of our teams get the same frameworks. A beginning team should have a more defined framework, while an experienced and successful team should be able to handle more space. In our organization, the experienced teams always run into terrain where they are unable to decide certain steps, and that frustrates them. The only thing is that you can't make different frameworks for every team."

"I understand that, Mark," Grandpa answers. "I didn't really have strong feelings about the cabinets. Three different sizes worked just fine. One cabinet for a small colony, one for a normal sized colony, and one for denser colonies. Three varieties were enough for me. Later we also got cabinets that could be expanded. If a colony worked very hard, we would simply adjust the cabinet in that way."

"Hmm," Mark thinks to himself. "I can do something with that. But how does it work when colonies split up? When do you adjust the frameworks? Who keeps track of that?"

"That was my job," Grandpa said. "That was my terrain. Monitoring the production of every cabinet, and deciding which colony should be in which size. That is the beekeeper's domain. If you call it a framework, then I was the one who set and adjusted them. Nobody else. And that was very intuitive. The decision to move a colony to a cabinet with more room needed to be made in a timely manner and with attention to their performance. They had to be producing through the roof for me to justify moving them, but it had to be done quickly because otherwise the colony would split itself up and there would need to be more cabinets anyway. In the end it was better to have many small colonies than several large ones. I could then also move cabinets around and see what happened if I moved them closer to a flowering field, for example. I would see how that affected the taste of the honey."

"And how does that splitting work then?" Mark asked curiously.

"Well," Grandpa explains, "I don't know if it's the same for you, but if a colony gets too big, then it splits itself. We call that 'swarming.' At that point the cabinet is too small for all the bees. One group of bees leaves and forms a swarm outside of the cabinet. Then you see this dense cluster floating next to the cabinet, they used to call it a beard. That's the swarm that you have to catch and move into a new cage. And then you have two colonies. That's how you grow your total bee population, year by year."

"Hmm," Mark mumbles. "That goes differently for us. We don't split teams up, we just start up new teams that work in tandem. The new teams are then quite different from the others and often have the tendency to reinvent the wheel. It always surprised me how some teams will spend months attempting to solve a problem that another already solved months prior. But they don't communicate. Luckily, I do have that oversight. I can partner them up or offer up the solution, which is often a lot faster. But maybe that's an idea that I can adjust. But letting teams split up once they are big enough, I would have to think about more."

Mark carefully takes a sip of his mint tea.

"But how does it work with those frameworks, Grandpa? I don't want them to be lopsided, having the authority of a dictator. It's much better if the teams think about it together. I can't imagine that you were able to discuss that with your bees?"

"Haha, no, not quite," Grandpa responds.

"But wait," Mark says, "It's probably like how it is with kids. Setting frameworks is also a part of raising kids. One recurring theme is always when you let them stay up until. Some kids will understand that it's not good to stay up late every night; it just makes you groggy in the mornings. At the same time, there is an equally unfortunate tendency to put kids to bed right after dinner; but that's too early. Clearly, it should be possible to find a happy medium. Half past nine, for example. And at some point, that time could be revisited. But obviously, there is a span of time where the framework is set and is not negotiable. Bedtime is bedtime, and if it's after half past nine there's no room for discussion. Never! Susan and I sometimes argue about it."

"Oh, why?" Grandpa asks.

"Well, Susan is too permissive. When there's a show on TV that runs fifteen minutes over, Mandy will always be allowed to finish watching. But somehow that seems to happen nearly every day, and so it goes. Before you know it you have the same argument every night. Mandy will have some reason every night, and with every exception you make the norm slowly shifts. For a kid, it will encourage them to argue back and push the limits, which I really hate. That's why bedtime is bedtime for me."

"I still don't know about that, Mark," Grandpa reacts. "In principle I'm following you, but at the same time there are exceptions. Imagine that something really special is on TV, like perhaps if you yourself make a brief appearance on a show, one hour past bedtime. Are you then allowed to stay up? Or if it's New Year's Eve or some other vacation day, then shouldn't she be allowed to go to bed later? It seems like every framework has its exceptions. I agree with you that existing frameworks need to be monitored strictly and not be brought to discussion when it's not timely. In that way they promote clarity. Frameworks are there to help when you need to adjust them. But they remain frameworks, so there can always be moments where they have to be adjusted. Later, during a calmer moment, when you have the necessary time and oversight, then you can discuss your frameworks again and see if the decision to diverge from the framework ended up being in everyone's best interest. To be honest, that's how it worked with my bees, except without their input," Grandpa remarks facetiously.

They slowly sip their tea, digesting their thoughts and looking out in the distance. Suddenly, Mark's phone rings; it's one of his colleagues. The tests carried out with the self-scanners look great and the project manager is asking permission to roll them out in all of the company's supermarkets. Mark asks a couple of questions and directs the manager to carry out some additional testing.

After hanging up, Mark puts his phone away and asks Grandpa another question: "How did it work when you were experimenting with new honey, by the way?" Grandpa sits up; he had been slipping in and out of sleep while Mark was on the phone.

"Yes, that was very important," he said. "Especially in the beginning, when I had hardly any experience, I had to try out a lot of things. 'Experimenting,' is that what you said? If you're doing something for the first time, then you have to continue trying it out. The quicker you fail, the faster you learn! Without experimenting, you cannot learn!

In the beginning, I didn't do that. I ended up treating bees like they were sheep. Small, fast, flying, honey-collecting sheep. But of course that's not the case. When I realized that I had to start from scratch, only then did I begin to experiment.

I can still remember," he continues, "that thanks to experimenting I learned very quickly what worked and what didn't. Especially which honey was better and what customers were willing to pay extra for. Lavender honey was a big hit. Deciding what new things to try, that was definitely my thing for a while; it is the domain of the beekeeper, after all. I decided where the cabinets would be set up, and the size of the cabinets, all that. I would place the cabinets within a certain distance of each other. Not too close, but not too far either. With most of my strategic decisions, I had to learn what worked and what didn't. As they say, 'Becoming a beekeeper is luck, but being a beekeeper is an art.'"

Mark replies: "You have a good point there, Grandpa. It definitely applies in my industry too. We work with so many new technologies and new services, and we never really know what exactly is needed and how we can deliver that; we are constantly learning. Sometimes it seems like we're doing everything for the first time. We still plan altogether and execute on the plan, even when we don't have the necessary knowledge to make a solid plan. We always start with the most difficult tasks, constantly experimenting, and less frequently learning quickly, which we don't do enough of.

But what I'm also thinking about is the importance of the environment."

"What do you mean by that?" Grandpa asks.

"Your bees are out there in the field, nestled by the flowers. Those are the beautiful valleys that I love to bike through. An environment like that makes you happy. It inspires! It really pales in comparison to our stuff office back on the mainland. Sheep you have to herd, because if you let them wander they will be gone forever, but that's not how it is with bees. Bees you have to let loose in an inspiring meadow full of flowers. Or even better: a nice meadow with blooming flowers provides a productive environment where the bees can do their work. The more inspiring the environment, the more people want to stay there! We don't pay nearly enough attention to that. Soon, we will be reorganizing our whole office; I think I'm going to advocate for some creative spaces that inspire and give off good energy!"

They drink the rest of their tea and walk back home. Grandpa goes back to house, and Mark walks in the direction of Aunt Ronda's house. Before dinnertime, Mark packs what he learned into a quick presentation. After a half hour, here is the result:

Lesson 3: Pick and Protect the Framework

- **"Laissez-faire" is not leadership**
  Pick and choose the framework, but let the teams inside the framework fill in the rest. Don't concern yourself with how things are being handled in detail.
- **Start with tight frameworks, and expand on them after hitting milestones**
  Beginning, inexperienced teams often need a tight framework, with a limited number of team members and frequent feedback to ensure rapid learning. Experienced teams that have demonstrated their capacity for success require broader frameworks and can collaborate better with more team members; essentially, they should be allowed to grow.
- **Frameworks are the guide, but the teams decide**
  Frameworks should not be brought up for discussion when you don't find it necessary. That's why they exist. As a leader, you protect the frameworks. If the situation commands it, you could diverge as you wish, but the framework should remain. You can evaluate later whether that particular framework makes sense and if it needs to be expanded upon, not as the issue arises.
- **Experiment constantly**
  By experimenting frequently, you learn faster what works and what doesn't. Without experimentation, you simply can't learn quickly. The more teams there are the easier it is to experiment. It's usually better to have many small teams than several giant ones.

Afterwards, Mark opens up his Outlook and responds to all of his urgent emails. All in all, he only needed an hour to get everything done. There are still some kinks with the self-scanners. They are from a different vendor than the cash registers, and the technologies are less compatible than expected. Good thing Mark ordered some extra tests earlier that day. He had suspected that there would be some problems. Mark passes along some tips to his teams regarding how they can best look for the solution. The second he puts his tablet away, Aunt Ronda calls for him from the kitchen; dinner is ready.

    He helps her carry some hot dishes over to Grandpa's house. Grandpa is fully prepared to eat, and has even already set the table.

6. Order, Structure, and Chaos

They eat schnitzel with potatoes and carrots. Chicken schnitzel, to be specific. Mark recognizes them immediately, they're homemade by Aunt Ronda of course. They are identical to the way his own mother used to make them, only a touch less flavorful. If she were here, his mother would respond to that by saying that she always makes them with love. Mark chuckles as he realizes that his mom's might just taste better because she uses salt and pepper.

Afterwards, Aunt Ronda brings the dirty dishes back over to her house. Mark stays over with Grandpa for a cup of coffee, but he did have his Auntie promise that she would wait with doing the dishes until he came back to help. She's old school, so everything will be done by hand, of course. "A dishwasher won't be brought in here on my watch," she always says. "Those things can only break. And also, I have the time to do it by hand."

As his Aunt lets the door close slowly behind her, Grandpa sighs: "Well then, now it's time for some real coffee!" He goes to the kitchen and comes back with two piping hot mugs and two empty cups.

Mark glances at Grandpa confusedly. Grandpa catches his glance with a twinkle in his eye, and says: "Here's your coffee! And I suppose you will also want a fresh glass of iced tea." From underneath the mound of newspapers, he fetches the teapot and carefully pours a bit of tea into the empty cups.

"Here, taste this," he says. "Tea for with the coffee!" And with a wink he takes a swig. Mark begins to suspect something and tastes it curiously. Cognac!

Now he understands why Grandpa didn't want Aunt Ronda emptying the teapot earlier that day. Aunt Ronda would never allow Grandpa to drink, but of course she would have nothing bad to say about iced tea. Grandpa is very aware of this. Mark chuckles, appreciating Grandpa's shenanigans.

"But Grandpa, isn't that bad for you?"

Grandpa responds: "Oh Mark, at my age it's alright every now and then. Not too often, though; with moderation! Like we used to say, 'he who drinks well bounces back well.'"

Together they enjoy their coffee, and of course their special treat.

"So, how is it going with your 'beekeeper lessons'?" Grandpa asks, clearly curious.

Mark explains that he's trying to put together a summary of what he's been learning, and that he's throwing a presentation together as well. He promises to bring his iPad next time so that he can show Grandpa what he ended up utilizing.

He asks: "But Grandpa, didn't the chaos of it all take some getting used to? Sheep walk together in a very orderly way, but bees fly in every direction."

Grandpa replies: "I did indeed have to adjust to that. At first glance, it always looks like a mess near the cabinets. The bees never fly in a straight line, and they come and go as they please. With my sheep, it was much more structured. That's when I realized; it always appears chaotic when the bees organize themselves.

But do you know what the secret is, Mark?"

"Well?"

"Nothing is as it seems. The appearance of chaos doesn't necessarily mean actual chaos. Indeed, you let them loose and have no idea exactly what they're doing. But looks can be deceiving. And in fact, there's more of a method to the madness than you would expect. When you look more closely, you see that everything is in fact in order. It is an orderly chaos, if you will!

Now take the inside of the cabinet. Have you seen how neat the honey trays are? Perfectly shaped hexagons all in a row, and all waterproof. Those honey trays are quite orderly. They're the first thing you look at, actually: the structure and quality of the result. That's what it's all about. That's also why I started saying that the bees revolve around the honey."

"Yeah," Mark answers, "that is indeed my first lesson: making sure to back out and scrutinize the result regularly."

"Exactly!" Grandpa exclaims. "With sheep you look at the flock, and with bees at the honey. The herd mentality is only predominant among sheep, and you can't expect bees to adopt it. The herd mentality just doesn't work for bees."

He continues: "There is however quite a bit of structure within a colony of bees. There's the workers, the protectors, and the drones, and each of those roles entail development and growth, even. A worker bee, for instance, starts by helping maintain the hive, then processes nectar in the cabinet, and feeds and cares for the larvae. Only much later on, when they are older, do they leave the cabinet to collect nectar from the flowers. It's not plain to see, but the order and development is there!"

"Interesting, Grandpa. I think I'm starting to realize that our company is organized as if it were a big flock of sheep, and that a beehive is much more complex. The structured chaos that exists as a result should not be rooted out, but should be encouraged," Mark remarks. His Grandpa looks at him smiling. It reminds Mark think of something else. "The bees also make it appear chaotic with those flow trajectories, those 'dances' that they do. At least, that's what I read somewhere. Is that right?" He asks.

"Oh yeah, I forgot about that," Grandpa says. "Yeah, you can see that really clearly when you take a window of the cabinet. But you have to know about it and be able to recognize it. I didn't know about it, and as a result I didn't see it in the beginning. I only learned about that later. But it is a good point you're making. There's more structure than meets the eye, and if bees need their own dance, then let them do it. Let them develop their own internal rules and dances."

With a firm tone of voice, he emphasizes: "Because the only thing that counts..."

"...is the honey!" Mark finishes his sentence.

"Exactly," Grandpa says. "Come here with that cup. One cannot walk on one leg; we might need another touch of 'honey' ourselves." He pours roughly a swig's worth of cognac into the cups. "Too much coffee can make you restless, but with cold tea you can sleep like a baby!" He says with a grin.

Mark thinks to himself that his teams also have 'dances' of sorts. Every team starts the day with a morning meeting. Some teams call it a 'stand-up,' and the technical teams call it their 'daily Scrum.' But it all boils down to one thing: a daily ritual that gets everyone on the same page, clarifying where things are and explicitly what is needed to solve the problems of the day. That does seem to resemble a bee dance, maybe. The only thing is that bees do it naturally, and Mark's teams have had to learn it themselves. Everyone's instinct is to just get to work and figure out the rest at the end. Telling how things are going in the meantime and asking for help are not automatic reactions. Bees are much better at that aspect.

Essentially, a morning meeting is nothing more than one of Grandpa's bees' dances, he thinks to himself. If teams need the dance to get their work done, then that's fine. In the end, it's all about the result anyway. Look at the quality of the result. From there you can see if things are going well or not. It's not the process that counts, but the result of the process: the final product. The honey-laden honeycombs show how well things are going.

Grandpa goes on: "But keep your hands off, eh! Respect the autonomy of the cabinet. That is their domain. Inside the cabinet, they are the boss, and they should be able to what is necessary and what they would like to do."

Grandpa raises his cup, and their tea cups clink as they toast them.

If Aunt Ronda had any idea…

***

It's already ten o'clock when Mark walks back into Aunt Ronda's house. The dishes have been done a while ago by the look of it. First, he makes a quick call to Susan. Their conversation is just going around in circles; she supports Mandy and her choice. Mark thinks it's all too sudden and half-brained. His anger has faded, but the current deadlock is irritating. And not only for Mark.

When Aunt Ronda invites him for a cup of tea, Mark immediately thinks of Grandpa's 'cold tea.' He smiles while thinking about Grandpa's sneaky little trick with the cognac.

He thanks his Aunt heartily, but says he has some work to do which leaves her disappointed. It's true though, he does want to keep working on his presentation. His conversation with Grandpa helped him develop his next lesson:

Lesson 4: Value the Apparent Chaos

- **Look at the result, not the process**
  Nothing is as it seems. Don't look at the looming chaos of the process; focus on the result. Try focusing directly on the result, and then extracting the result through iterations. If the quality of the final product is good, you can leave the minutia of the process to the teams. In the end, they are the ones responsible.
- **Rituals offer a mainstay**
  Teams have the own ways of obtaining a given result. These distinct strategies, principles, dances, and rituals are their own. Do not meddle.
- **Keep your distance, but remain in the loop**
  Fight your instincts; don't involve yourself simply because things appear to be chaotic. Look at the result, and the structure and quality of that result. You can intervene, but only if the final product isn't good and the team isn't doing anything. That is precisely when you must intervene; if the team doesn't deliver good results, you're the one on the line.
- **Encourage incremental learning**
  First ask questions, and then help in a constructive manner. If that doesn't work, narrow the framework, or make the decision to change up the team or end the project. Help the teams learn to solve issues themselves.

It is now half past twelve when Mark shuts off the light in his old, trusty bedroom. He had actually wanted to revise his email and listen to his voicemails. Still, he noticed that he's beginning to internalize the lessons and that he's warming up to the prospect of letting his teams figure things out themselves.

Now he just needs to make sure that they are going to understand it back at home, and that Susan and Mandy will realize that they're on the wrong side of this one.

Tomorrow is yet another day, he thinks to himself. The long day has knocked him out, and the alcohol is doing its work as well. Within a minute, Mark is fast asleep.

7. More by Doing Less

At half past five, Mark wakes up due to the natural light filling his room. The window is wide open, and a crisp breeze circulates inside. Because it was so dark the night before and due to his fatigue, he forgot to close the curtains.

He slept quite well, and he can even peek outside the window from his bed lying down. A clear blue sky. Despite the air being a touch crisp, it promises to be a great day.

Mark gets up, pulls on his hiking boots, and heads outside. He crosses through the village to get to the water. First he walks a few miles along the dikes, but he decides to veer off to the left near the creek, so that he can walk to the other side of the island through the forest. The beach appeals to him more than the dike. When he arrives at the beach, it's still fairly calm.

One beach shack is already open for business. A man sits there on the terrace, reading a newspaper. He's decked out in a full suit. Mark walks onto the terrace and looks for a spot in the sun. This early in the morning, it's actually quite nice to feel that warm sunlight on your face. The owner of the beach shack is busy sweeping. After about fifteen minutes, he walks over to Mark and lets him know that they're not open yet. The man sitting on the terrace with the suit on, it turns out, is actually his father. He just became a pensioner and is struggling to adapt to a new way of life. That's why he comes to his son's beach shack quite early, every day. Even though they're closed, the owner says he can have a cup of coffee in the meantime. In an hour they will be fully open, and Mark will be able to order breakfast.

A wonderful start to the day: having an early breakfast in the summer sun on a terrace by the beach. Mark feels very fortunate. What more could a person want?

***

Around ten o'clock, Mark returns to Grandpa's house. Grandpa had just finished reading the newspaper. "Ha, hey there grandson," he exclaims. "So, did you sleep alright?"

"Like a baby!" Mark replies. "And you?"

"Great. I feel like a young buck!" He winks: "But our little sleeping aid will stay between us, right?"

"Of course, Grandpa," says Mark, winking in turn: "Only next time I'm going to ask Aunt Ronda if she wants a cup as well."

"Oh just leave it!" Grandpa retorts. "She would only get worried. She already has a hard enough time sleeping. No, you shouldn't make those kinds of jokes, Mark.

But where is that computer of yours? Weren't you going to show me what you've been working on?"

"Oh yeah, sorry Grandpa, I did say that," Mark responds. "But I still have some questions. It's not done yet. I don't feel like we've covered all the bases and I want to finish it before I show you. But to be honest, it's a shame to be sitting here inside. It's really nice weather, and not too warm either. I actually want to propose that we go outside. I had breakfast this morning on the beach, and it was lovely! So come on, get out of your chair. We're going to the beach. Maybe we can grab some lunch there, too."

"That sounds great," Grandpa replies. And so they ride towards the beach. Of course, Aunt Ronda insisted that Grandpa wear the canary yellow scarf, and the shepherd's staff protrudes out of the car like an antenna.

***

They walk from the parking lot through the dunes to the beach shack. It's barely doable for Grandpa. His staff provides ample support, but Mark is still alert just in case. If Grandpa falls, Mark will be ready to catch him.

"So what did you want to ask?" Grandpa inquires the moment he takes his seat at the table. "What have we not discussed yet?"

"Well, Grandpa, with the bees you cared for several distinct colonies and placed them in different locations. On the one hand, I understand that, but on the other, couldn't you have just left the cabinets near your house? After all, the bees do the work and you would be able to harvest faster and more easily."

"No, No, No, oh Mark..." Grandpa says, shaking his head all the while. "You still don't get it, huh? You still don't see what everything revolves around. It's not about the beekeeper, but the bees! Hence the saying: 'the song of the bees is more important than the song of the beekeeper!' Yes, of course it would have been easier for me to place all the cabinets right next to my house. But not for the bees! And since they are the ones doing the work, that's more important. They have to fly further, which takes time, and so you get less honey. And besides that, the more colonies, the more flowers you need, which means that each bee needs to go even further. That doesn't work. Flying is wasted energy! As the beekeeper, you have to identify these problems and take them out of the equation. The less time the bees waste, the more honey you get.

But my job as a beekeeper was to find out how my bees could produce more and better honey. That means looking for new fields, or trying something with a specific honey by closing one cabinet, for example. If the final product was less than favorable, then it was my job to look for the cause. The bees can't identify the cause themselves; otherwise they would've fixed it already."

"I don't understand that last part, Grandpa," Mark says. "What do you mean when you say: 'if they could remove the cause themselves, they would've already done so'?"

"Look, Mark," Grandpa replies, "You have to really trust that it's in the bees nature to work tirelessly. That they really do their best. They do everything within their power. They even clean their own cabinets! So if the honey does disappoint, you have to find out why. It's never the bees; they always do their best. But clearly, something is getting in their way. What that is and what needs to be done, that's your job! Sometimes they get irritated in the forest, so you have to move them to another area. Other times, they get bothered by a nearby farm, or the cabinet is too exposed to the sunlight or is on a slope. It's different every time. There will always be problems that the bees can't resolve themselves. A good beekeeper stays in tune with what's bothering them, but never argues with the bees' input. Not only when there are problems, but also when things are going well!"

"Yeah, I know that one," Mark says. "Because it can always be better!"

"Exactly!" Grandpa says.

Mark thinks back to the Lean Program that was instituted in his company. All of the managers and executives were trained in Lean and had to learn all kinds of techniques to identify waste. Waste reduction was the magic bullet. There's always going to be waste, and you have to find it and cut it out. Flying, like with Grandpa's bees, was a type of waste within Lean: 'transport' was what they called it. In principle, those ideas from Lean weren't so crazy. It was just difficult to keep the focus on the right thing. The first projects were very straightforward, and they were able to identify the waste no problem, but in the course of time, it got more complicated. At that point, the mantra was "it can always be better!" But because it had to happen in addition to everyone's existing workload, it always stayed in the background. Mark is still quite impressed that his own Grandpa, who has never heard of Lean before, came to similar insights using his intuition and observations as a beekeeper and shepherd.

But Grandpa emphasizes once more: "You have to trust that your teams want to do their work and that they're always doing their best. That trust must be inside of you. Only when you have that trust can you find the causes of problems. Like when my bees were sick, for example. Usually it was due to a parasite in the cabinet, which I would rectify. But that didn't take out the root of the cause. Where did the parasite come from? If I discovered that, and I was able to remove the source, only then would the problem truly be solved. You always have to look for the problem behind the problem. That's what you have to fix, because the bees can't do it themselves."

Grandpa continues: "It took me a long time before I understood that. My job as a beekeeper was no longer to concern myself with the bees' work, but to ensure that the bees could carry out their work to the best of their abilities. And that is much harder. As the saying goes: 'there are as many bad colonies as there are beekeepers.' It's never the bees' fault. It's always the beekeeper! I had to learn so much more. About mold, illnesses, parasites, and honey quality. And you know how much I love reading! Not really though. Maybe the newspaper, but do you ever see me reading a book? But it was necessary. You also learn from visiting other beekeepers. That was a little harder here on the island, since I was the only one."

"Yeah, but Grandpa, couldn't you go to that other beekeeper? To that brother on the other island?" Mark inquired.

"Go off the island? Are you crazy? I already get homesick when I sit on a boat in the harbor. No, I didn't do that. I didn't really feel like it."

"And there was nobody on our island who also kept bees?" Mark asked.

In one way or another, that was precisely the wrong question. Grandpa was already stirring a little in his chair. Mark noticed him slouching more and more, with his back to the terrace. As if he was hiding himself. Now he's almost sitting sideways; clearly, the question made him feel uneasy.

"Well, Mark," he responds with a subdued tone of voice, "I had to do everything myself. Only later, when William came, did things really change." Suddenly, his tone becomes more harsh, and he retorts: "But I don't wanna talk about that!"

Mark decides to leave it at that. He did promise Aunt Ronda he wouldn't pry, after all.

***

They order lunch. They both get an omelet on brown bread. Grandpa should be eating salt-free bread, but it's alright this once, he insists. Mark takes his omelet with ham and cheese, but Grandpa lays off due to his special diet. Still, Grandpa doesn't seem to be at ease. He seems nervous. Very unusual for him...

They eat their lunch in silence.

"Sorry to interrupt," says a soft spoken fellow, right when Mark takes his last bite of his meal. "I just heard your voice and thought that I heard Mr. Vandenburg. It's you, isn't it? How are you?"

The man stands behind Grandpa. It's the beach shack owner's father. He's got a different custom suit on this morning, with a matching tie of course. Even the watch is different. Grandpa doesn't look up. He's busy having the last few bites of his omelet sandwich.

The man continues: "Don't you remember me? It's me, Will Rust!"

The unwelcome guest extends his hand towards Grandpa, who is mid-bite and looks away to the side. He seems torn about what to do. Then he chokes on his last bite. He coughs and coughs, turning bright red. Mark gets up and gives him some firm pats on the back. The other guests look on, clearly concerned.

Thankfully it passes quickly, but Grandpa still doesn't look too good.

"I didn't scare you there, did I Mr. Vandenburg?" The unexpected visitor says. "I don't look that scary, do I?" He once again sticks out his hand.

"No, not at all," Grandpa grumbles, ignoring the hand reaching across the table.

"How are you?" The man asks. "It has to be at least 30 years..."

"Yes, that's true," Grandpa replies curtly. He's irritated. "35 years to be precise! Back then you didn't have such a nice suit and expensive watch! But you probably don't remember that, huh? You probably forgot about that with all that money of yours!"

But before the man could react or Mark could offer the man a seat at their table, Grandpa says: "Come on Mark, let's go. I don't feel well, so I'm going to go." Grandpa stands up, grabs his staff, and walks away without saying a word, leaving behind Mark and the unexpected guest, who were both quite flustered.

Mark has never seen him walk that fast.

His eyebrows rise up, and he looks at Will startled: "What's his deal?" He asks.

"Oh, let it be," Will replies. "Mr. Vandenburg and I know each other from way back when. We have kind of a history. I honestly thought that it would be far gone memory by now, but I guess not."

He continued: "Go on, go after him. Don't worry about the check, I'll take care of it. Lunch is on me!"

And with that, he walked back inside before Mark was able to respond to his offer at all. Mark sits at the table confused. He wonders what happened in the last few minutes. He stands up and heads toward the exit.

When he steps off the terrace and onto the beach, he sees Grandpa's staff disappearing over a dune in the distance. He looks back at the beach shack and sees the owner standing next to his father in the doorway. Mark waves goodbye, and Will gestures in Grandpa's direction. Even though he doesn't understand what just happened, he heads out.

***

As they leave the parking lot in their car, Mark asks Grandpa: "What was that? What was that all about? We're just having lunch and then suddenly you leave!"

Grandpa says somewhat indifferently: "Don't worry about it. I choked and didn't feel well. That's all. It was just too warm there, and I want to go home. It's time for my afternoon nap!"

"Come on, Grandpa," Mark says. "That's nonsense. You skip your afternoon nap all the time. Be honest. What happened there with Will? You know him from back in the day, right?"

"Pffff...Will!" Grandpa exclaims. "Always trying to be hip, that guy. It never stops. He used to go by William, and now it's Will. That moron, he hasn't changed at all!"

"Was that the William that we're not supposed to talk about?" Mark asks surprised. "He said that he knew you from back in the day, and that there are still some sour grapes."

"Did he say that? Sour grapes? Unbelievable!"

"But what happened that made you so angry when he seems completely fine?"

Grandpa reacts irritated: "Because he's a secretive slimeball. That's why! And he was back then, too." And then with more emphasis: "But didn't I say that I didn't want to talk about it! I'm going to close my eyes, because I'm tired!"

Grandpa closes his eyes and crosses his legs rigidly. Mark decides to leave it at that. He promised Aunt Ronda that he wouldn't talk about William with Grandpa. And given Grandpa's reaction, he's already asked too much. Not that there was anything he could do about them running into William spontaneously, but still.

Mark tries to enjoy the sun on the quiet trip back to the house. Last time, Grandpa fell asleep as well, but this time Mark gets the feeling that he's very much awake. Yeah, he's pretending to be asleep, but that's not the same.

***

When they arrive back home, Grandpa swiftly gets out of the car, mumbling some gibberish, and goes straight into his house. Mark has a seat at the kitchen table in Aunt Ronda's house. She's not home.

He decides to work on his presentation. Apart from the incident with William, they did discuss the removal of hindrances as being the most important task.

Lesson 5: Removing Barriers

- **Trust in the team's knowledge**
  Trust that the teams will do everything in their power to obtain the best result. Teams want to work hard. When the results disappoint, it's never the team's fault. Don't blame them, trust them, and look for what's holding them back.
- **Look for the underlying causes of problems**
  Teams have no issue solving simple problems. But finding the underlying cause and removing it is your job. Look for the barriers that they don't see themselves or can't solve themselves. They need your help with that.
- **Minimize distance**
  The smaller the distances, the less waste. Put teams close together and ensure direct contact with the client. Give teams a window into the value that they are providing. Streamline feedback loops and let the teams observe the impact of the changes.
- **Keep looking for improvements**
  Even when things are going great, there will always be barriers and hurdles. Remove them, and the result will get even better. The teams will take care of that!

When Aunt Ronda stops by later on, Mark tells her about the encounter that Grandpa had with Will earlier. She sighs and says: "Oh, Mark, don't worry about it. I already read that William sold his company. I've never heard Grandpa speak about it, and I've never asked. However, he does read the newspaper cover to cover every day, so he's definitely read about him; the fact that he's become so wealthy probably is what's bothering Grandpa. I honestly didn't think that he would return to the island. He goes by Will now, huh? Yeah, that's typical for him. And sure, there are plenty of people who change their first name, right? " She winks at Mark.

"But Auntie," Mark answers. "What's the tension between him and Grandpa about?"

"Well, it's a long story and it's somewhat petty. Don't you know how it goes among men? Sometimes they think they're both right, which might actually be the case. But they don't understand themselves, that they can both be right."

She continues: "But I have to go do some groceries for dinner tonight. I'm way too busy. When I have some time, I'll tell you the whole story. But be careful, okay! Don't mention anything to Grandpa! It really winds him up. And that meeting today, he won't be too pleased about that. His health is more fragile than you think, and he needs to sleep well. I think I might actually stop by the Doctor real quick to get some more sleeping pills for him. He will probably need those."

She gets up, heads for the door, and leaves the house by bike. Mark stays behind at the kitchen table. Again today, everyone is avoiding him and leaving him confused. He is still somewhat shocked about what happened on the terrace. He still doesn't get it.

Who is William? What's the story there? Why is this such a sensitive matter? Why can't it be discussed?

Suddenly, he realizes that there is one more person who might know more. And that person would talk about without reservations.

Mark gets up, puts on his biking gear, and grabs his mountain bike. He bikes there at a high speed, along the shortest route.

8. Getting Stung

It's already around dinnertime when Mark gets back to Aunt Ronda's house. He's been gone all afternoon and had a long conversation in which he was able to ask all of the questions he had.

A lot became clear to him this afternoon.

During dinner, there's silence at the table. Aunt Ronda is not very talkative, Grandpa even more so, and Mark has a lot on his mind. After dinner, Grandpa doesn't invite Mark over for coffee, so Mark stayed behind and helps Aunt Ronda with the dishes. But Aunt Ronda doesn't volunteer any information and Mark doesn't really have any questions to ask anymore. They wash the dishes in silence and Mark goes for a late night walk under the starry skies. The moon shines brightly over the island, giving it a sort of magical hue.

Then, when he's nearing the end of his walk, he approaches the village and takes some time to recuperate on the bench across from the old town hall. The moon illuminates the building's white facade brightly. Mark thinks back about what might have happened here. He tries to picture himself there, and can almost see it all unfolding around him like in a film. He thinks about all the decisions that have been made here and all the political games that have been played. He has no clue, or he's not sure; either way.

When he gets home, Grandpa's lights are already out and Aunt Ronda has also retired for the evening. He ponders adding another lesson to the introduction of his presentation from earlier in the afternoon. He decides against it. He needs to discuss it with Grandpa first, he thinks to himself.

And with that thought, he goes to bed. But not before he writes Susan a text message: *"Can we talk about Mandy tomorrow? I have thought about it and have a plan! XXX"*

After that, he puts his phone on silent mode and quickly falls asleep.

***

The next day, Mark wakes up bright and early as usual. Given the late night he had the night before, he uses the first hour of his morning to fire off some emails. It's not too bad this time. Only one more test until the self-scanners can be deployed at all of the company's supermarkets. He doesn't call Susan; she always has little time in the mornings and what he wants to discuss will take more than a couple of minutes.

Then he goes for a stroll near the village and is the first guest in the old town hall tea room. He notices that he feels restless. He wants to go see Grandpa, but he doesn't know how that will be. He needs to spare Grandpa from the ordeal of talking about William, and he promised Aunt Ronda as much. But now that he's spoken with William at length, does that change things, or not? Would he be able to bring it up without Grandpa getting wound up?

***

It's quarter to ten when Mark heads over to Grandpa's house. He hasn't been awake for long, it seems. He's walking around in his pajamas, which Mark has never seen him do before. He looks very tired.

"Good morning Grandpa," Mark greets him.

"Well hey there!" He sighs: "Oh man, I'm exhausted. I slept terribly and was just tossing and turning. I kept falling asleep and then waking up only a couple of minutes later. I'm dead tired. I need coffee. You as well?"

"Certainly!" Mark replies. Grandpa pours them each a cup and warms his hands on the piping hot mug.

Mark starts the conversation: "So Grandpa, I've been looking at my notes, and I want to talk with you about ego."

"Ego?" Grandpa asks. "How do you mean?"

"Well, look. As a shepherd, a lot was dependent on you. You indicated that you were one of the best shepherds on the island-probably even the best. And then you became a beekeeper overnight, and had to start again from scratch. That must have been hard on your ego...I mean, how could it not be?"

"Oh, like that," Grandpa responds as he starts explaining. "Yeah, that's definitely a thing. The bees take care of everything themselves, and your role completely changes. And that does affect your ego. You do get stung every now and then, for instance. But that's a part of the job. It's annoying for you, but even worse for the bee, which will die. That's why you have to aid them in not wanting to sting you. And you can't blame the bee for stinging you. Bees sting, and usually it's your own fault because you're not paying attention. You have to accept the fact that bees can sting you, but you can't sting them back. As they say 'if you want honey, you've got be prepared to get stung'!"

He continues: "So yeah, ego does play a role. Everyone can see that you're the best shepherd, that you have the largest flock, and that you lead your flock that best. But it doesn't work that way for beekeepers, who are working in the shadows so to say. You're busy fixing problems and increasing production, but at the end of the day, any compliments are for the bees; they're the ones who make the honey after all!"

Mark listens to what his Grandpa is telling him. What he's saying about getting stung is interesting. It makes him think of his workplace. There are certainly some team members who 'sting,' but with words. And there are those who can't keep their mouths shut. Especially the software engineers. They are so quick to get angry, and when they are angry, it ain't pretty! Sometimes things get so heated and personal that it's impossible to make amends after a given outburst. With some people, that leads to an irreparably fractured relationship. Not literally, like when a bee dies, but it does lead to people jumping ship. It's too bad, because they're really good at their jobs. Is that comparable to a stinging bee who would rather not sting, but dies when the inevitable stinging takes place? Mark doesn't know for sure, but he does appreciate the principle.

He probes further: "Yeah, but how about beside that, Grandpa? Apart from the bees. What did it do to *you* to no longer be the best shepherd on the island? That you and your flock were no longer ubiquitous? Surely that must have been difficult?"

Grandpa thinks about it, staring straight ahead, and then says: "Well, maybe a little. In the beginning I of course got some great compliments for the honey. I still had a long ways to go, but still. They asked me to do it for a reason, and I felt honored. It only went haywire when William came. Or Will, as that sly old fox is calling himself nowadays. William ruined everything. It's his fault that things went the way they did!"

"But then what happened exactly?" Mark asks curiously.

Grandpa sighs deeply. "Mark, I don't want to talk about it. I already told you that. Please don't press the issue. That whole thing made me so restless last night!" He shrugs his shoulders.

"But Grandpa, I think I already know most of the story," Mark says. "Yesterday, I spent the whole afternoon talking with William and he told me about that time. He also said he understands why you are mad at him."

"Of course he understands," Grandpa retorts. "Thanks to him I lost all of my work, despite that fact that I was the one who taught him everything he knows."

Then he gets noticeably angrier: "I'm disappointed that you're being so nosy about this! My own grandson, spending time with that traitor. I hope you had fun!" Grandpa is furious.

Mark responds: "Come on, relax. I understand that you're angry, but please try to look at it from my perspective. It's all William's fault, but then when I ask about the details, nobody will say a thing and it's taboo to discuss it. Is it really that surprising that I went to ask him myself? You and Aunt Ronda are completely silent about it. And besides that, you're talking about a traitor, but every story has two sides. Maybe it would serve you to hear him out. It's too easy to blame everything on someone else!" Now Mark finds himself angry at his Grandpa's stubbornness.

Grandpa sighs deeply and sits in his chair. He rubs his cold hands together. The silence is palpable.

Then he starts to talk again: "Okay, Mark. You have a point. You've now heard his side, so now let me tell mine."

Grandpa proceeds to tell the story. It's mostly identical to the story that William described the day before.

William was a young guy who didn't do too well in school. Upon his mother's request, Grandpa had given him a summer job to keep him busy. The summers are busier for beekeepers than the winters, so Grandpa could certainly use another set of hands.

William had no experience whatsoever. Not with bees, but not with sheep either! He was therefore much better at learning how to keep bees than Grandpa. He constantly asked questions about why Grandpa did things a certain way, but Grandpa didn't do well with criticism. "This is the way I've always done it, and it works, so that's how we'll keep doing it," was the answer that he usually gave William.

Admittedly, William wasn't the best pupil at school, but with the bees he made very astute observations.

He had asked Grandpa for a small colony for himself, and Grandpa had obliged. Things exploded from there on out. In the following years, he built an empire like you wouldn't believe. First with honey, and then with all sorts of biological products, with accompanying storefronts spread all over the country. Mark even recognized the brand. Susan and he regularly shop at BioRust. Mark hadn't made the connection between William's last name and the company name.

On the island, during the first few years after his vacation job, things went very well with William's honey. It only took two years for William's production to exceed Grandpa's. And it was better quality product, too. After a few years, Grandpa's operations were suspended by the island council, and honey production was exclusively done by William.

Grandpa was thanked for his contributions over the years, but he was no longer needed as a beekeeper. He had tried after that to herd a flock of sheep once again, but to no avail. His experience with the bees had made him worse at herding sheep. He gave the sheep too much space and didn't train his dog well. Essentially, that meant his career came to a quick close, and he went on early retirement.

Grandpa was left empty handed as William became a millionaire. All this despite that Grandpa, out of the goodness of his heart, had helped William along. He still blames William for that. William had offered Grandpa a job in his company, but Grandpa's pride led him to refuse.

William told Mark yesterday that he can understand that. He assured Mark that it really was nothing personal, as far as he was concerned. He also said he didn't have a choice. Grandpa had beekeeping down to a science, but William just ended up being faster and more handy in the honey business. And of course, William had not been a shepherd, so he went into the experience with a fresh mindset and learned much faster. After all, the island council had put him under pressure to take over from Grandpa eventually. It wasn't his fault that it went so well that he was able to place cabinets all over the country. His company had the momentum of a cargo train, and it was always going to continue chugging along. That it was William specifically who would be in that position, seemed entirely coincidental; thing just ended up going that way in the end.

Grandpa finishes his story: "That's it. That's my story. I still can't believe the way it all went down. I feel abandoned by the island council, and cheated by William. I was the laughing stock of the town. So yeah, that definitely messed with my ego. Quite a bit, actually! They used to tell the story of the American dream at school: from paperboy to millionaire. That's how it felt for me, but in the wrong order!"

Mark doesn't know what to say. He sees how Grandpa really takes it all so personally, and it makes him think about himself. He's important in the company. He's the Fire Chief putting out all the fires, the superhero who you can always ask about something if nobody else knows. He's on a pedestal. Is he okay to step off of it? Can he let go of his ego? There's one thing Mark knows for sure after hearing the story of Grandpa and William: if he can't let go of his ego, he's not going to make it. It's about the team, not about him.

Grandpa announces that he's going to go back to bed. He's still tired from his restless night. Mark bids him farewell, and goes to his room to fetch his iPad.

Lesson 6: Let Go of Your Ego

- **No ego**
  Self-managing teams have no need for a manager with an ego. The final product is more important than your ego. Get your satisfaction from the value you offer your customers, client satisfaction, and the independence of your teams. The result is the only thing that matters. Measure it; it's what determines your new ego.
- **Any culture change begins with you**
  You are still important. But now, you put others in the spotlight instead of yourself, namely your teams. You will have to work on yourself as well to do things differently than before.
- **Embrace criticism**
  Welcome criticism, even if it hurts. Appreciate all feedback, recommendations for improvement, and complaints. Anything that improves the final product helps. Often, criticism is a consequence of not paying attention, which is your own fault.
- **Pass all compliments along to your teams**
  If it went well, it's because of them, and if it went wrong, it's because of you. Give compliments in the presence of good results, and encourage your teams to continue improving themselves.

When Mark finishes typing, his phone's backlight illuminates. He had set it on silent mode when he went to bed last night, and had apparently forgotten to turn the ringer back on the next day. Fifteen missed calls, he sees on the screen. He calls Joyce right away.

There's all sorts of problems. The cash registers aren't working in any departments! Mark tries to get to the bottom of it by asking questions over the phone, but he realizes quickly that it's quite a crisis. It has to do with the self-scanners and the adjustments that were made to the cash register's interface. Now nothing works anymore, not in a single department even. While he's on the phone, he checks his email on his iPad and sees four emails from the CEO.

This is a huge issue. The grocery store customers are not able to check out in any of the company's supermarkets! This is the biggest crisis Mark has seen. Bigger than that time when customers could only pay with cash.

Mark quickly decides to take the next boat back to the mainland. He looks for Aunt Ronda to explain to her that he needs to go back to the shore, but she isn't home. Mark leaves behind a note for her, stating that he's rushing to the office and will be in touch.

He puts on a suit and the dress shirt that he wore on the way to the island. It was only a few days ago, but it feels like it's been weeks. His dress shirt smells great. Aunt Ronda washed it, of course. Maybe she's even more caring than my own mother, he thought to himself.

***

It takes two full days before all the cash registers are up and running again. In most stores it only took one day, but there were some where it took two. It ends up being the biggest crisis that Mark's company has ever faced. The CEO is extremely concerned and is micromanaging everyone. He keeps emphasizing how much the disruption is costing the company every hour. He wants report after report. The effect ends up being that everyone is too busy writing reports or answering questions instead of actually working to solve the problem.

Maybe it's good that Mark went back to the office. His first move is to shelter all the teams who are solving the problem from the proverbial storm. After that, he stays at the office for 48 hours without sleeping and does what he's always done. He keeps thinking about the lessons he wrote down on the topic of self-managing teams. But that's for later, he thinks to himself. First solve the crisis, and then we can work on the culture.

In essence, that's what he learned on the island: a real switch to self-managing teams is a complete culture change. And the change lies in each individual. In this crisis, he can only lean on the current culture, which thankfully he knows how to navigate. Change will come eventually.

**

That evening, he collapses on the couch at home, freshly shaven and showered, much needed after those two consecutive days at the office. He's exhausted, but happy that he got the job done.

Mandy doesn't waste any time cutting to the chase. "Dad, I'm dropping out of school. No matter what you say. I am enjoying working at the hospital so much. It really is what I want. And mom agrees with me, so..." Susan hears what her daughter is saying and walks to the couch, saying: "Mandy, hold on a second. Your dad says that he has a plan and I think that we should at least hear him out." Mandy mumbles a confirmation.

Mark suppresses a deep yawn. He's more exhausted than he thought. But after all that discussion about personal development on the island, he knows that this would be the first moment since being back to discuss it at length. He explains again that a diploma counts for something, and that you can always fall back on it in the future. Mandy looks bored, staring at the ceiling. At the same time, he acknowledges that he understands where Mandy is coming from. He proposes: "You know what we'll do. How about you just take a gap year. You'll have to finish this school year, of course. But it's only two more months."

Mandy grimaces. Duh! That was her plan all along.

Mark continues: "Well, in that gap year, you can pursue that program you want and work at the hospital too. Then you'll get extra work experience, which can never hurt. Then you can go back to school, because a one year break isn't the worst thing. And if you've had a great year and enjoy the program, you can always decide to continue with that. In essence, you would be giving yourself more time to make up your mind. What do you guys think?"

Susan seems conflicted. In her work, she always advises people to not make 'half-decisions.' At the same time, she also sees that this is quite a compromise for Mark. She knows how strongly against all of this he is, but he's still giving Mandy a year to decide what she really wants to do. She says: "I think that sounds good. What do you think, Mandy?"

Mandy begrudgingly agrees, but not before adding one thing: "But I know for sure that I'll just continue with the program. I know that this is what I want to do!"

When Mandy goes up to her room, Susan asks Mark why he relented in the end. Mark replies: "Well, I had some good conversations with Grandpa. One of the topics was 'ego.' To be honest, I wonder if it's my ego that's holding me back from embracing this. Not only with the educational program, but also in my own job. I think I just want Mandy to get her high school diploma and go to college - so that she'll get a title. But maybe that's more for me than for her. I'm not sure about it, hence my proposal. Let's let her experiment and find out if it's a good idea, and then I can figure out if my resistance is due to my ego."

Susan smiles, gives him a hug, and kisses him. "The vacation brought you more than some relaxation, it would appear," she says. "Was Grandpa coaching you?" Mark responds, smiling: "Maybe a little bit," and then adds: "but I coached him too!"

Before Susan gets a chance to ask Mark if he can't just admit that he was wrong and that it could be due to his ego, the house phone rings. She walks over and picks it up. After a few quick replies- "yes," "okay" - she gives the phone to Mark, who is already half asleep on the couch. "Here, it's your mom. She has bad news."

Mark's mom explains that things aren't going well with Grandpa. He's feverish. The Doctor stopped by, and it looks like Grandpa has a lung infection. He should go to the hospital, but he doesn't want to. He doesn't want to leave the island. He's getting antibiotics and oxygen, but it doesn't look good.

9. Back to the Island

It's almost a month later when Mark is back on the ferry. Not on his way to the island, but on his way back to the mainland. Susan and Mandy are with him this time, but the reason for that isn't pleasant. They had just finished burying Grandpa. He was already quite old, and at that point things can deteriorate very quickly. All in all, he was sick for about three weeks, through which he kept getting weaker and ultimately passed away in his sleep. Aunt Ronda was with him.

Mark had tried to visit Grandpa the week before, but unfortunately it didn't work out. It was too busy at work. And also, Grandpa was incredibly weak. He couldn't even scale the stairs anymore. For that reason, they had to move his bed to the living room. Aunt Ronda showed Mark a photo from that time; Grandpa looked frail and tired. Mark did notice that the bed was right next to the kitchen table, and that if Grandpa stretched out his arm, he could reach his special teapot. He didn't mention it to Aunt Ronda.

It was a beautiful funeral. Living to be 93 years old is of course quite special. Still, Mark had a knot in his stomach. After those great days that they had shared together just a month prior, it all came to an end. And it's a shame that he was never able to share his presentation with Grandpa. If you wait to show something until you know it's perfect, it can often be too late.

Mark did feel guilty and wondered if his visit was too exhausting for Grandpa, but Aunt Ronda was adamant: "No, Mark, those three days with you were some of his best days in years. He really enjoyed it. He mentioned it quite frequently these last few weeks. No, that he got sick has nothing to do with you. It was just time."

She continued: "And look at me. I worried myself sick all these years about his blood pressure and his heart. That was his weakness, and I tried to protect him. But you see, there's not much you can do about these things. In the end, it was a lung infection that ended it. Who would have known?"

**

As they were headed back to the boat, Aunt Ronda ran after Mark: "Wait, Mark!" She had a plastic bag in her hand. "Grandpa asked me to give this to you. Here!" For a moment, it seemed like she didn't want to let go of the bag; the transfer seemed to take just a second longer than what would be typical. Mark looked at her, and then she released the bag into his hands.

"But hurry along now, get in the car," she then said, "otherwise you'll miss the boat!"

On the boat, Mark walked onto the deck with the bag. Susan looks at him with a concerned gaze, but he winks to let her know that he's okay.

In the bag, there's a large white envelope. Mark rips it open. A crinkled, handwritten manuscript falls out of the envelope. It's his Grandfather's notebook from when he was a beekeeper.

An old teabag pokes out as a bookmark. Mark opens the manuscript there. On the last pages, there's a message scribbled in Grandpa's characteristically sloppy handwriting.

Dear Mark,
Things are not going well with me, which you will have heard by now from your mother or Aunt Ronda. You and I didn't get to finish our conversation. Calling won't work anymore since I am too nauseous, so I'm committing it to pen and paper.
Your visit was fantastic! I really enjoyed touring around the island with you, and visiting all the places I hadn't been in years. I loved telling you stories from my day, and trying to help you with the changes you were planning on making. But in hindsight, I think the thing I appreciated the most was that you helped me look at that situation from the past in a different light.
I have harbored ill-will towards William for years. For far too long, I thought that the problems I encountered in my life were his entire fault. Only now, after our conversation, do I see that I should have taken ownership myself. I just was never able to be as good of a beekeeper as I was a shepherd. I used to be the best shepherd on the island. And I couldn't let that go. I never had the courage to take that next step. That's why what worked for me with the sheep didn't work with the bees; I didn't give it my all.

And for a shepherd, it's even more burdensome to become a good beekeeper. Learning begins with unlearning. To learn something new, you have to be prepared to discard the old thinking. And as soon as it starts to get really difficult, you go back to what used to serve you well. Letting go of that which once worked is perhaps more difficult than learning what does work now. Change is inside you! If you yourself do not change, then nothing actually changes. In short: the worst way to become a great beekeeper is perhaps by being a shepherd first. Or as we used to say: don't bother teaching an old dog new tricks!

You helped me to realize that the more my ego got in the way, the slower I changed and thus the greater the chance becomes that life passes by. I changed, and I learned, but because of my ego it went very slowly. And then you end up trying to handle bees like you handle sheep. Please don't copy me in that way, Mark. Make a real decision. To become a beekeeper, you have to change. Not only in words, but also in actions. And that change lies not in the bees or in the sheep; it lies in you! Choose what suits you best, and go for it!

With warm regards,

Your grandfather, Marcus Vandenburg,
                occupation: Bee-Shepherd.

Mark carefully closes the fragile manuscript, and presses it tight to his chest, closing his teary eyes. But despite the tear going down his cheek, a confident and satisfied smile begins to form. Mark knows what he needs to do.

He has made his choice.

The Bee-Shepherd Model

In many organizations, employees are mobilized to perform tasks like they are flocks of sheep. Many things are decided for them, down to the smallest detail, even though they are capable and intelligent themselves. They even end up building the most intuitive systems. Leading these teams successfully asks more for the approach of the beekeeper, and less for that of the sheepherder and his dog. Out of this came the idea that a shepherd can't lead a colony of bees without a complete change of approach.

The lessons in leadership that the story of Mark and his Grandpa illustrates can be summarized in the *'Bee-Shepherd Model'*. The foundation of this model is a personalized process of change initiated by you as a leader. You should be aware that all prospective changes are entirely in your hands. In the end, the changes are within you, and never in another.

The model therefore builds strongly upon this foundation, to the extent that you're always looking to improve and appreciate new learning experiences.

```
        LEARN
         AND
       IMPROVE

      COLLECTIVE
       CULTURE

   SELF-MANAGING TEAMS

    RESULTS IN RHYTHM

     TRUST AND LET GO

   YOUR PERSONAL CHANGE
```

The model has six layers:

1. **Every change is within you.** Look first for the change in yourself. If you don't change, then nothing will ultimately change. Do this by looking for pain points, going against your intuition or gut feeling, and unlearning the old way of doing things. Look for the things that you're proud of, and determine to what extent those things could have been stifled under the old paradigm.

   For example, think about "Yeah, but…" constructions; weigh them in your head. It's okay to not have all the answers. It's good to experiment and try new things. It's not a problem if you don't know exactly what your people need to do, as long as you know when it will lead to the desired outcome. Think about the analogies of the shepherd and the beekeeper and sheep and bees; see if it can help you. What would a great beekeeper do? When you need to make decisions, or when you need to think of new ways to direct your team, the analogy can help. In the end, you are the manifestation of what the change is, and so your personal process of change is the foundation of the model. And you don't change through words alone, it's really the actions that count. Saying and knowing that things need to change is one thing, but implementing real change is another. If you're not ready to change your behavior, then why would your team? Appreciate also that un-learning is also a process of learning. What do you need to un-learn?

2. **Trust by letting go.** Never doubt the team's competence; that is the basis of trust. Never blame an individual team member for something. Look for the causes that underlie the problems you encounter, and identify the learning experiences that arise from problems you solve.

    Don't meddle, and definitely don't meddle in the operational side of things. Make teams responsible, but never, ever, take back the responsibility. And watch out, because the devil is in the details: an approval of a decision, a request for advice.

    Think back to the analogy of the shepherds and beekeepers and ask yourself: what would a beekeeper do? If what's happening looks like something a shepherd or dog would do, then it's probably not the right choice.

It is important to make it abundantly clear how things are going. Being transparent with results and the way in which goals become realities is key. If it's not clear whether or not a team is successful, then it becomes more difficult to get there. Make the goals and outcomes transparent and trust that your teams will execute.

Letting go does not mean that you can't intervene; you just do it in a different way. You intervene in the selection of teams. You intervene if the results are unsatisfactory. You intervene when nobody takes responsibility. But remember: intervention should always be focused on the future. You create a new situation in which teams can organize themselves. You change the context in which they operate. That's how you move forward. Honing in on past mistakes and their perpetrators doesn't yield anything. It won't improve things, and it will not be fun either.

3. **Delivering results consistently.** Make the results transparent for the client, and establish a clear delivery rhythm. The value you are offering the client should always be the mainstay. And clients don't like waiting for results, they want them now. That's why you establish a rhythm and flow of delivery and work. Look at Scrum for example, and the one to two week sprints that it recommends. The shorter the cycle, the more nimble you can be. And also, shorter cycles mean faster progress, implying faster learning

and improvement. An established rhythm prepares you for unexpected events, because you can tackle new problems immediately in the next cycle. In many cases, you will have to work with short cycles. Each cycle yields a working, valuable result for the client. It's all about the honey!

Make the outcome and its value completely transparent, even though it might not be easy at first. The more frequently you deliver results, the faster you learn and improve and the more you get motivated, because the teams will see the value in their work. Delivering results is fun! The more results you deliver, the more motivated you will become.

4. **Autonomous and self-managing teams.** The more bee colonies, the more honey. Each colony takes care of it all. For that reason, grow and scale teams that can operate independently of each other. Again, use the analogy of the beekeeper: bee colonies don't pass work amongst each other, but take care of everything themselves, from blossom to honey.

Each team must therefore have its own specific form of direction. Inevitably, it should be pointing toward the result: your job is to provide direction there and to make the results transparent (along with the value it offers the client). For the rest, the direction should be determined by implementing and preserving frameworks at the team level. Defend the frameworks, and let the team defend them too. And remember: every exception to a framework paves the way for additional exceptions. Despite the pain that may arise, decide upon a framework and stick to it. At a later, more calm time it can always be brought up for discussion, or an exception can be established. But at the moment the framework starts yielding good results, it should not be brought up for discussion. If you do that, then there will effectively be no true frameworks.

This only works well if you work with short cycles. In a long cycle process, there is no room or opportunity to reflect, later on, upon how to change the framework. In a long cycle process, frameworks are usually pushed to the side when there is a crisis; which makes the framework a farce. In short cycle system, rules are only adjusted during moments of calm, and as an experiment to see if things can be improved. Thus not out of necessity, but out of a potential to improve.

5. **Continuously build a collective culture.** There is no room for ego. The client and the team's needs should always be the main drivers. Everyone works as a part of a collective team, and the team works on behalf of the client. The manager has an important role in this: providing a vision, setting goals, removing problems, but foremostly curating a collective culture.

Root out egotistical behavior. In a team, there's no place for celebrity behavior. The needs of the collective are always more important than those of a single team, and the needs of the team are always more important than those of an individual. Far reaching transparency helps the cause drastically. Work tempo, productivity, and value delivered should be made clear and transparent. Measure those metrics regularly and hang the overview on the wall. And celebrate the accomplishments of the team, or what has been accomplished collectively. You can often see a collective culture in the small details. Do you clean up others' trash they left out when you go put away your own? Is everyone ready to do grunt work when it's needed, and is the janitor accompanying the team on company outings?

For a leader, it's important to not want to be in the spotlight yourself, but to constantly put others in the spotlight. For successes, compliment the teams who have outdone themselves, let the teams evaluate each other, and so on. In everything that you do, you must be aware of how it contributes to your desired collective culture. Every action must be a confirmation of the desired culture.

Reward desirable behavior in your teams and keep in mind that compliments are only beneficial if they are linked to the result. This is an important one. Before you know it, you could be complimenting their approach, and in that way you would be meddling in the operational flow. Focuses on the process, which is precisely what we don't want to concern ourselves with. Better is: "Fantastic result! What can we learn from this?" Praise your teams when the results are great, and make sure to help underachievers see how they can get there too.

Even as a leader, you won't be in the spotlight, but don't forget that your actions are scrutinized microscopically. Processing feedback and criticism is a part of that and offers learning opportunities. The way that you, as a leader, deal with work, serves as the example for how the teams will do it. Learning and improving is the priority and making mistakes, experimenting, and getting feedback and criticism are crucial to the process. Become an expert at breaking down criticism and digesting feedback and converting it into actionable items. That's the right example to set.

6. **Never accept the status quo: it can always be better.** Improvement is a never ending process. You must embody this notion, and show it in your own actions. Stability does not exist: things get better or they get worse. The status quo is the past. The market, the client, and the context are always changing, so if there is no improvement, things are getting worse. In your role as a leader, you must hone in on that: remove barriers, blocks, and waste and institute a culture that encourages experimentation.

That last part is especially difficult for many people. From elementary school onwards, we teach children that they are not allowed to make mistakes. We engrain that in them for twenty years. Then they go work in a dynamic environment, where they can only learn precisely by making mistakes. That leads to cognitive dissonance, and it doesn't work. "Wanting to try" is integral in encouraging quick learning. You must make mistakes! As many as possible, and as quickly as possible; make as many mistakes as you can. That's how you learn how to avoid the real problems. And even a big problem can be a learning experience.

Trust in your teams, and let them make mistakes. Also look inward: didn't your biggest learning experiences come from times that you made mistakes? Why would you not wish that type of learning upon your teams? And lastly: un-learning is an integral part of learning. What works now, might not necessarily also work tomorrow. What didn't work before, maybe could now. For that reason, continue experimenting. As a leader, you have a lot of influence: don't accept the status quo. Things can always be better, and that's why you should always strive to the next phase of (almost) perfection.

Do you need to implement every part of the model?

Yes and no. It is not an absolute, complete and entirely closed model, but it can help you discover what you need to do; to figure out where the problem is. In fact, if a certain aspect of the model is not implemented, the consequences are fairly predictable.

- If you aren't striving towards improvement, then you get stagnation, demotivation, and decay.
- If you don't cultivate a collective culture, then you get a dysfunctional organization in which the client's needs are at odds with the individual needs.
- If teams don't manage themselves, then you need considerable overhead and coordination, otherwise the teams deteriorate into chaos and get burned out.
- If there isn't a transparent result and there isn't a rhythm or flow, then you get discussions and ad-hoc results, and your teams lose their focus because they can't tell if they're heading in the right direction.
- If teams are trusted and aren't set loose, you get failure to make mistakes and dysfunctional teams that cannot independently bring out their best qualities.
- If you're not constantly striving towards personal improvement and change, and instead look outward for change, then you get dysfunction. Real change comes from within. From inside you. There's only one person who can make it happen, and that's you!

Another way to lead

Depending on the independence-level of the team, you might need to adopt a new brand of leadership. Beginning teams require a different type of direction than highly experienced teams. Isn't it much more complicated, then? Well yes, of course it is! From a leader in an organization with self-managing teams, many more leadership skills are expected than when teams are managed by command and control. With self-managing teams, the responsibility lies at the team level, and thus leadership will have to be more flexible and will have to shift gears with agility, implementing varying leadership skills and tactics.

Even more importantly, developing a self-managing team requires coherent leadership vision. The frameworks for results should be clear and follow a set rhythm. On the other hand, self-management has no place for frameworks that attempt to define how work should be done.

Your task as a manager is to cultivate your teams to be self-managing, by constantly focusing on the result and cycles. "We have two weeks, and I want a working result, no matter how small." In meetings: "You have ten minutes, and then we expect a decision!" In workshops: "You have eighteen minutes, and then we expect a summary of the lessons you learned." The time pressure, in tandem with the expectation of a given result, compels teams to organize themselves effectively. If teams don't know what they need to do, then nudge them in the right direction and remember: "they are not fully independent yet, so they do need further development." Now that is leadership.

Because who doesn't want to help others improve?

Epilogue

More and more, I see managers and other leaders wrestling with their role when they work with self-managing Agile teams. I see them fret about what they are and aren't allowed to do, and also when they should or should not intervene. I think that the analogy in Mark's story can lend some help: what do you need to do when you want to transform from a shepherd into a beekeeper?

You can't treat teams like sheep; you have to let them do their thing. Just like bees. Trust that they will execute, especially when things aren't going as planned. What you have to do is extract the honey and help them to solve their problems! That motivates them.

Deliver results quickly, learn what works and remove obstacles. If teams can quickly get an idea of what clients value and what they don't, then they get a better feel for what they need to prioritize.

The analogy of bees and self-managing teams was not something I invented. My colleague at the Delft University of Technology, Professor Erik Meijer, pointed me to a blog post called "How Software Companies Die" by Orson Scott Card, in which he discusses 'beekeeping software engineers.'(*) He posits that self-organization behavior of software teams has many parallels with that of bee colonies, although the leadership rarely ever emulating 'beekeeper tactics' to do it.

Often the term 'self-direction' is used instead of 'self-managing'. In this book, we use 'self-managing' though. This is a deliberate choice. A bee colony does not direct itself; a beekeeper directs it. The beekeeper determines where the cabinets are placed, and of course the spatial organization of the bees. The notion that teams don't need direction is a myth; they need goals and frameworks. You direct them with those very goals and frameworks. Thus you create a context, a playing field, and then you let them figure out the rest- after they've been directed, of course.

In our daily job at Prowareness: executing client transformations to working with self-managing teams, the changing role of management is always a theme. I have had to learn what this change is like and how it works. In my first transformations, I made the mistake of neglecting the management. I thought: it's all about the teams. But that is not enough: in the end the managers are the responsible party. Therefore they comprise a key part of the change.

At the same time, we can't prescribe how to change managers' behaviors. We as consultants cannot dictate how to think and handle things, and how not to. That works only superficially, and (if it were possible) would only be temporary. For managers too, the change has to come from within.

It's becoming increasingly clear to me how to adapt the analogy of the beekeeper and how a manager can transform from a shepherd to a beekeeper. It is an absurd exaggeration of reality, but for a manager in an organization that moves to switch to self-managing teams, this analogy could well be the solution. An adjunct tool to test, inspire, direct, and measure the effects of new behaviors.

Thus this story came to exist. The lessons come from experience, but the narrative is entirely fictitious. Which island is it? Who knows? As far as I'm concerned, it only exists in the imagination, just like the main characters. And Mark's company? That doesn't exist either, although it is likely to resemble many real-life organizations.

And Mark? Does he exist? Yes, he probably does. Everyone knows a Mark, even though he might sometimes be called Bart, Gerald, Maria, John, or Chris.

Otherwise, look in the mirror. Ultimately, the change that Mark undergoes is one that we undergo as well. In you, and in me. Eventually, every day we will have to look for a piece of Mark in ourselves and will have to decide if we want to be shepherds or beekeepers.

Use Mark and Grandpa's lessons. Fill in your own as well. Ultimately, it's about the leadership lessons you internalize, not Mark. Mark's Grandpa has already showed us that real change lies within. If you and I don't change, then ultimately nothing changes.

Undergo this change consciously and take the time for it. But remember above all that you can only learn by experimenting! The only way to learn faster than someone else is to make more mistakes, more frequently. Even in a politically sensitive environment, where big mistakes are highlighted and punished, experimenting often is not a bad idea. The best way to avoid most large mistakes is namely to make lots of small ones.

I wish you every success, and hope that you will share your experiences!

Rini van Solingen
Zoetermeer, The Netherlands, September 2, 2016.

(*) http://www.cs.cmu.edu/~chuck/jokepg/joke_19970213_01.txt

Acknowledgements

You never write a book alone. I want to thank the following people:

- Erik Meijer, for showing me that software development teams have more in common with bee colonies than with flocks of sheep.
- Jos de Blok, the author of the foreword. His organization, Buurtzorg Foundation, is world renowned and a shining example of how concrete goals can be reached faster and better through self-managing teams. Jos, thank you for your contribution and your kind words!
- My colleagues at Prowareness, who helped me with detailing the precise roles of an 'Agile beekeeper': Ron Eringa, Jeroen van Menen, Jan-Pieter van den Heuvel, Henk Jan Huizer, Rob van Lanen, Stephan van Rooden, Michiel Vrasdonk and all the other Prowareness colleagues who contributed their stories, knowledge, and experiences.
- The reviewers of the early versions of this manuscript, for their critiques, compliments, and suggestions for improvement: Mark van der Zwan, Svenja de Vos, Teun van der Vorm, Eelco Rustenburg, John Numan, Amir Arooni, Ronald Dähne, Theo Geelen, Marc

Gill'ard, Peter Groen, Johan van Hall, John Heideman, Frans van der Horst, Henk Jan Huizer, Martin van Langen, Peter Noordzij, Dick Stegeman, Alfred de Vries, Pieter Weterings, and all the other reviewers who I may have forgotten above. I also especially thank those who provided their review for the first two pages of this book.

- I also thank Stefan Stettler, who contributed what he has learned through his role as a project manager and as a board member of the Beekeeping Club Mergelland, and helped me to sharpen my limited knowledge of bees and to correct factual inconsistencies in that arena. Any faults that remain are entirely mine.
- I also am indebted to all the directors and managers who I have had the privilege of working with over the years, who inspired me and have showed me how to effectively lead self-organizing teams in practice: Amir Arooni and Nilguin van Raad (ING), Arie van Deursen (TU-Delft), Ate Lindeboom (CRV), Dick Stegeman (CMG en IHomer), Emiel Romein, Ronald Dähne en Aad 't Hart (Exact), Phil Brown (Causeway), Pieter Zwart (CoolBlue), Svenja de Vos en Frank Klomp (Tele2), Teun van der Vorm (ANWB), Tino Scholman (Oracle), Vikram Kapoor (Prowareness) and many more.
- Additionally, I would like to thank those who shared their struggles with me and have showed me precisely what does not work. These lessons were perhaps even more valuable because they inspired me to actually go and write this book.

- John Numan, for his continued trust, welcome criticism and feedback, and daring to publish this book in the Netherlands. Thank you as well to the entire team at Business Contact Publishers.
- Roelof Grootenhuis for the English translation and reformatting the story for an international audience. Anna de Waard-Leung for helping me out with the final questions.
- Finally, I want to thank the home front: the rock solid backbone of my life. Thank you for your stimulation and support. Without you and you guys, I could not be myself, and I could not do what I do. ♥

About The Author

Rini van Solingen is a part-time professor at the Delft Institute of Technology. At TU Delft, he teaches and conducts research revolving around globally distributed software teams.

Additionally, Rini is the CTO of Prowareness (www.prowareness.nl). There, along with his colleagues in The Netherlands, Germany, India, and The United States, he helps organizations work nimbly and deliver high-value software products. Leadership of large scale Agile transformations and implementing Agile with tens or hundreds of teams is his specialty.

In addition to Prowareness and TU Delft, Rini is a volunteer at Logeerplezier, a charity organization that he started with his wife Patricia. Logeerplezier provides vacation homes and getaways for handicapped children and their families.

In 2010, Rini wrote the bestseller "The Power of Scrum" (along with Jeff Sutherland and Eelco Rustenburg), in which he explains Scrum in narrative form. In 2014 he wrote "Scrum for Managers" (together with Rob van Lanen), to assist managers to direct teams in an Agile framework. Both books have also been published in German and Dutch.

Rini is contactable via r.vansolingen@prowareness.nl, d.m.vansolingen@tudelft.nl, or rini@rinivansolingen.nl. Don't hesitate to contact him with any questions or to discuss a topic. He enjoys hearing from you and (mostly) responds faster than you might expect.

If you want to do him a real favor, invite him to do a lecture, training, or to present a workshop. That is namely his biggest passion.

> Did you enjoy reading this book? Are there any others you might know, or might you yourself be looking for a custom version of this book, in the style of your organization? Or do you want to help translate it to another language? Please don't hesitate to initiate contact via email to the following address: rini@rinivansolingen.nl.